Dwelling

Dwelling

Living Fully from the Space You Call Home

Mary Beth Lagerborg

Revell
Grand Rapids, Michigan

Published by Fleming H. Revell
a division of Baker Publishing Group
P.O. Box 6287, Grand Rapids, MI 49516-6287
www.revellbooks.com

Printed in the United States of America

Library of Congress Cataloging-in-Publication Data
Lagerborg, Mary Beth.
    Dwelling : living fully from the space you call home / Mary Beth
Lagerborg.
        p.   cm.
    Includes bibliographical references.
    ISBN 10: 0-8007-3207-3 (pbk.)
    ISBN 978-0-8007-3207-3 (pbk.)
    1. Home—Religious aspects—Christianity. I. Title.
BR115.H56L34 2007
248.4—dc22   2007003230

In keeping with biblical principles of creation stewardship, Baker Publishing Group advocates the responsible use of our natural resources. As a member of the Green Press Initiative, our company uses recycled paper when possible. The text paper of this book is comprised of 30% post-consumer waste.

green
press
INITIATIVE

For Alex
my home mate

And for Mimi
who dwells well

Contents

Introduction

The Home Tours Begin

We all want a home base where we are accepted and rejuvenated. Where we can lick our wounds, create without censure, give and receive love, have fun, and rest. Where we can be cared for when we're sick and age with grace. Where we can eat and drink and sometimes be merry. Where we can be our best and be our worst but always be moved toward our full potential. We all crave this sort of home.

Each of us brings with this desire the measuring stick of our experience in our own home of origin. For better or for worse, that is where our stories began. There we were shaped, wounded, loved well or not well; we developed our tastes, our preferences, and our prejudices. We remember favorite meals and holidays and family gatherings, or maybe we remember loneliness or sarcasm or sandwiches alone in front of the TV.

If we grew up in a healthy home, the memories are rich and sustaining. And since we know what is possible in a home, we long to create it in the new context that is home for us—

whether that is an apartment or someone else's basement or our dream-home-come-true.

If we grew up devoid of any satisfying sense of home, with a hunger for "a real home," we're hoping our vision is not a mirage that is hopelessly unrealistic and unattainable.

The bottom line is that the place that was home to us, and the relationships that were shaped there, mattered. They mattered in our past, and now they matter in our present and our future. You recognize this, and you care about creating a healthy home. That's why you're reading this book.

Just as your own home mattered for you, your efforts at creating home will make a difference. Those differences will be largely immeasurable and intangible, and yet at times you will see, as if a curtain has been opened, positive influences of home that have your fingerprints all over them. The satisfaction you'll know is gentle and deep.

Your home, wherever it is now or later will be, is alive with possibilities to provide wholeness and health—and fun! This book will help you decide what you most value in your home. You will be able to spot what's missing and address those things.

Throughout the book you'll hear from many people who live in a wide variety of circumstances but all share an appealing sense of home. They will share what they've learned from situations that were pivotal in shaping the personality and healthiness of their homes. At the end of each chapter we'll actually visit in a home or two. These "home tours" will give us glimpses into the inner world of these homes. We'll explore what these people have learned and experienced that will be transferable and beneficial in our own quest to create home.

If you glance at the table of contents, you will see that topics related to making a home include an "inside" and an "outside." The topics in part 1 deal with the personality, the atmosphere, the warmth, and the internal support systems essential to the place we want to call home. These topics are addressed inside our homes, often with "just us." But a home functioning at its best also prepares and motivates us to participate in the larger world and to welcome people into our homes. So part 2 will explore how we can extend the shelter of home into a larger sphere.

Imagine yourself along with me sheltered within four walls that represent key concepts of home: One wall represents to us that home is a physical structure, an atmosphere; another holds the thought that home is also the relationships developing inside that structure. The final two walls encompass our need to cocoon, draw in, and be ourselves and our need to participate wholly beyond our walls and invite other people to share the experience of what we have within.

Come with me in and out of the homes of others. You will celebrate the home that you have, its people and its possibilities, and move onward in creating the home you long for yours to be.

Red House

Dear Pat and Ron,

I know that I have never been quite able to express my feelings about the Red House, I suppose because they were a combination that escapes definition. You see, it was not only the love of the house itself with its setting, its long history of family ownership, its every physical inch, so to speak, but something more than that . . . the fact that always there was love inside the house, love not made evident by overt signs simply but recognized by intuition and the heart, and that has been a resource on which I have drawn all my life. A combination, as I say, quite beyond words, but which perhaps explains why, when I had to leave the house I felt that I could never go back—

Anyway I have to write to tell you both that Ruth and I came away yesterday feeling above all that there is the same combination in your house—your home—something transcending the skill and work and perfection of what you have done with the physical house. And so you both have done something immeasurable for my spirit.

—Richard Warren Hatch, last Hatch family owner
of Red House, built in 1611, New England's
oldest continuously lived-in house[1]

Building Inside

Part 1

Whoever
you are at home
is who you are.

Jeff

A Place to Be Me

As I round the bend and our house comes into view, it doesn't matter whether the grass needs mowing or the driveway needs shoveling, or even that the empty trash barrels—if it's a Tuesday—are tipped over in a jumble out front.

I pull into the driveway. The drawbridge goes down. I drive in. The drawbridge goes up. I enter the house. Sigh. I'm home.

After greeting family members and Gus, our standard poodle, who is bouncing off the ground on all fours, I head upstairs to change. My at-home uniform waits on a hook just behind the closet door. The soccer pants are the extremely comfy kind with a cotton layer inside and nylon outside. They have a small hole in the left knee from my falling down in the street and, most importantly, an elastic waist. I add a T-shirt or turtleneck and sweatshirt depending on the season, cotton socks, and felt slippers smashed down at the heels.

No matter what the day has been like, now I'm all better. I'm at home.

Home is first and foremost the place where we are accepted, where it's safe to just be. It's a place where it's okay to not wear makeup and where cereal will work for dinner if that's what you have it in you to fix (or to let others fix). Don't we all crave such a place?

Thumbprints

People say that home is an extension of ourselves. I agree. It is the place with my personality thumbprints all over it. It's where my personal tastes are developed and enjoyed. Our home has a perennial garden because I like the blooms but with minimal work. Mr. and Mrs. Alligator salt-and-pepper shakers sit on the table because my son Tim picked them out as a gift for me and I like them a lot. In the family room a (new!) large, comfy, red leather chair and ottoman is so "mine" that I keep a favorite magazine lying open there to reserve it. The next time I can sit down, it's waiting for me to read, and none of the big guys around here will dare prop his shoes or smelly socks on that ottoman.

Yes indeed, our home is an extension of my personality, and it's where I am most me. But it's also where my husband Alex is most Alex and where our oldest son Tim, currently living in the basement, is most Tim. So sometimes those personalities play thumb wars. How can our home be home for all of us?

The Christmas season is a time in our household when personalities regularly collide. Several years ago my husband Alex and our youngest son Drew took on the outdoor lighting "design." Each year it grows and grows as they incorporate new finds from garage sales, Wal-Mart, and, yes, neighbors' trash.

The best addition was a nativity scene that they cut out of plywood and painted. It includes a kneeling Mary, a kneeling Joseph, a wooden manger with wooden halo, and a wooden star of Bethlehem into which they poked enough holes for a string of white lights. The holy family is centered in the low evergreen shrubbery between two aspen trees, with the star hanging from one aspen. It is lovely, understated, enough.

Ah, but there is no "enough." They've been joined on the house and in the front landscaping by strands of large- and small-bulbed multicolored lights, flashing white lights, tiers of icicles, strands of blue lights, large red orbs. A plywood Rudolph with red light-bulb nose stands on the mailbox. A lighted wreath hangs over the garage, and two greenery wreaths purchased annually from Boy Scout Troop 554 grace the front doors. This year Alex found a gold bandana that he thought would look good balled up to form the head of baby Jesus—until he noticed that it said "Miller High Life" on it and dropped the idea. Our son Dan refers to the total scene as "Mary, Joseph, and baby Jesus in Vegas."

One year I asked them if they didn't think they should draw up a plan before they started decorating. They looked at each other. Alex said, "We have a plan. More is better." Drew nodded.

I think simple is better. Understated is better. So I proposed a plan: how about if they handle the outdoor lighting however they want (they always did anyway) and I handle the inside decoration?

They agreed. They still help decorate the Christmas tree, but I halted the inevitable progression of "more is better" to the inside of the house. They enjoy their annual creative project on the outside, and I enjoy simpler decorating inside. We each get to add thumbprints where they most matter to us.

Understanding Our Differences

Once we understand the personality traits of those we live with, we can develop plans that take into consideration and respect the needs of all. Although I'd like to think differently, there is really not much that is truly right or wrong about these things—just differences in tastes and ways of doing things. If we take the time to understand how each other is wired, we can more easily extend the kind of acceptance that we ourselves want to receive.

Have you ever sat outside a supermarket and watched the people entering? Mom invariably carries a toddler or preschooler or grips the child's hand as they cross the parking lot. If she has too many children with her to handle, she corrals them in a shopping cart.

Dad, on the other hand, lets his toddler scamper through the parking lot in front of or even behind him—or he totes the child on his shoulders. And inside the store he's more likely than Mom to let the kid explore free of a restraining shopping cart.

Daddy style and Mommy style often differ at home too. Maybe Daddy likes lots of structure in the family schedule, but Mom likes to wing it. Daddy thinks Buford the dog should sleep on Jake's bed; Mommy thinks that's terrible. Both parents care a lot about what's best for the family and the home, and they may be tempted to think that their style is best, or even that their style is "the only way." If one parent doesn't accept the style of the other, clashing Daddy and Mommy styles can create conflict or friction at bedtime, or during Saturday-morning errands, or when Mom's away for a weekend and Dad's in charge. The truth is that children and homes are enriched by both styles. Neither is more right; they are different. (The exception, of course, is where one parent's style is definitely unsafe for the child.) The trick is to recognize and then enjoy the differences, compromising here and there, to smooth acceptance of each other at home.

Home is a place where we want to not only be accepted but also flourish and grow. A proverb says, "Train a child in the way he should go, and when he is old he will not turn from it" (Prov. 22:6). Scholars tell us "in the way he should go" means "according to his bent, who he was created to be." In other words, if we can unlock the mystery of a child's personality traits, talents, and aptitudes and encourage these, especially at home, then when he is old he'll be functioning on all cylinders. And he'll be easier to live with along the way!

Kathryn is a mom with five sons, one of whom is emotionally fragile and an introvert. For this son they developed some special family rules. He has his own room (not all the older brothers do), and family members must knock to enter if the door is closed. They must also ask to borrow his things. Life goes better in their household when they do this. As Kathryn explains, "We need to know the other person well enough to know what they need from us. . . . You don't have to change who you are to become them. You can step toward the middle and make a plan."

In another family, nine-year-old Chase is visually challenged. Sometimes he has a hard day on the playground or in seeing his schoolwork. He can't wait to be in the car headed home. When he gets into the car he asks his little sister, "Caroline, what are we going to play today?"

"Home is a refuge," says his mom. "It's where he can be normal and accepted. He's comfortable and not stressed out. It's his sanctuary, where he's fully accepted and he can be fully loved."

It takes effort on Chase's mom's part to create a refuge for Chase. Structure and routine help him. "He's good about it," she says. "He knows he has to get in bed on time because his eyes get tired. For him there needs to be an order, a routine. I don't want him to feel like home is haphazard, crazy, where he has to take the responsibility to always fend for himself. When he leaves for school I want him to know his lunch is packed, he's had his supplements, his homework is done. I want him to feel that that part of his life is organized, ready to go."

This mom feels satisfied in knowing that she can provide this refuge where Chase can be himself and thrive and also be prepared to face a challenging outside world. "He's really smart," she said. "And I just want him to be able to always put his best foot forward." Chase can, because he's totally embraced at home.

Communicating with Each Other

Since I also want so badly to be accepted at home, I need to communicate my needs so that my family members understand and can help me "be me." Once I had a roommate who had a mannerism that really bugged me. But it wasn't as if she was doing anything wrong, so I kept it to myself.

Finally one day she said to me, "Look, I know that something I'm doing is bothering you, and if you don't tell me what it is, it's not fair to me, because I don't know how to deal with it." She was right. To keep channels of communication open, we need to tell our family members or roommates what's really bothering us.

Of course, verbalizing what we want doesn't automatically mean we're going to get it. Sometimes it means conflict. That's okay, because home is a laboratory where we learn to disagree and to work our way out the other side of a disagreement. To healthfully disagree is a crucial life lesson that we learn at home, largely because at home we let our hair down—we feel safe.

Soozi, who is a therapist and a mom, says that "it's devastating to hide conflict, because the children grow up having a gut sense of one of two things: either they believe they grew up in a perfect home and discover later in life that they don't have the skills they need to handle conflict, or they become bullies. If you come out from closed doors to the dinner table," Soozi continues, "and the kids never see how you got from the explosion to the dinner table, it just creates confusion. Allowing a child to observe adults struggling with each other produces in the child the awareness that adults struggle and work it through. We stay connected even though we disagree. There may be things we just agree to disagree on. We respect somebody else as different than ourselves."

Showing respect includes the manner in which we talk to each other. We can so easily slip into sarcasm or mumbling, especially if this is what we're hearing a lot. I consciously tried to pattern the way I talked to my boys after how a friend talked

THE ROUTINE

Our family had a special bedtime routine: After story time and lights out, Alex or I would rub each boy's back in the dark as we'd talk and pray with them. They would share much more—and different things—in the dark, with a soothing touch, than they would have told us eye to eye in the light. The boys welcomed the routine well into their teenage years, until they went to bed after we did. There's something magical about the combination of a backrub, quiet conversation, and prayer that gently coaxes communication.

to her children, because her tone was always so positive, and I wanted to sound more like that. Otherwise, I defaulted to a tone that sounded spookily like my own mother's voice.

While riding in the car one day with my husband Alex and our oldest son Tim, when Tim was a baby, Alex said to me, "You sure talk to him nicer than you talk to me." Ouch. It is easier to talk sweetly to the cutest baby in the world than to your husband. So it's important to be conscious of our own tone of voice. Am I speaking to family members in the way that I would want them to speak to me?

Double Listening

One morning when Drew was a preschooler, he and I sat on the front stoop listening for his school bus. "I think I hear it," I said. "Do you hear it, Drew?" Drew put his ear up against my ear to see if he could hear what I heard.

I call that double listening, or listening intently to another. Getting to know one another at home requires double listening—giving eye contact, getting on a child's level and really listening, not facing the TV while talking. Listening is important for all ages. My friend Mimi says, "If you don't listen to a toddler, you won't listen to a junior higher." Kids get ignored, overlooked, and misunderstood a lot at school, on the playground, and in childcare. The one place they should know they will be heard is in the safety of their own home. For that matter, adults need double listeners too.

Turning on the Porch Light

Once I'm at home and changed into my magic comfy clothes, I go down to the kitchen and pull from the cupboard my favorite glass (a unique one so I can identify it as mine on any table in the house). I pour myself a concoction of two-thirds iced tea and one-third lemonade or cranberry juice, walk to the front hall, and switch on the front porch lights. My transition is now complete. I'm "in" where I belong.

But mixed into my own sense of well-being is the realization that my family members are also "in" to a place where they belong just as much as I do.

Home Tour: Safety Net for a Single Mom

When Steph had a baby in her midtwenties, without marriage or support from the birth father, her parents invited her and her son to live with them. Steph saw this as a step backward in some respects, because she had lived on her own for several years. Her parents had gotten used to being on their own too.

The first year was the hardest, as they struggled to establish the roles of three adults and a child in the home. But with time and the settling into roles and life routines, Steph found a safe place to get used to mothering and to sort out how to be a single parent. The arrangement gives her some relief from financial strains and probable frequent moves. And she values the support network for her son: having a grandpa as a male role model, a grandma to pick him up from childcare, and both to provide consistent love for Sean—and for Steph.

They're all firm on the fact that Steph is the parent. At times Grandma or Grandpa needs to act as a parent because they are caring for Sean. But when Steph gets home, she takes over, and her parents don't challenge her methods or decisions. "They don't overstep. They're hands-off. They want me to be the parent," Steph says.

Their living arrangement requires good communication and respect for each other's needs. Little by little Steph has decorated her room so that although the bedspread and curtains belong to her parents, the wall decorations and photos around the room are her own. In Sean's room Grandpa, who is an artist, has painted a canvas for the wall with the trains that Sean loves.

Steph had assumed that she and her son would stay for only a year, but that year has stretched to six. Now she is employed full-time, Sean is entering kindergarten, and she's ready to move on, to find a home of their own. Surprisingly, that impending separation is proving as hard on her parents as on her because of their attachment to Sean and their concern for how tough life can be "out there." In addition, Steph says—and she thinks her parents would agree—Steph and Sean living with her parents has kept her parents younger.

Steph is looking for a home where Sean can play; a backyard is especially important to her. And for herself she wants a comfy chair where she can curl up with a blanket around her, a cup of coffee, and a good book. She's looking for a new safe place.

Home Tour: A Friend for Dusty

Alice is an extraordinary woman. My earliest memory of Alice is from the time she persuaded her husband Dale, who is a dentist, to wire her mouth shut to help her lose weight. Seated at a meeting table with a dozen women, Alice consumed milkshakes through a straw wedged between her teeth and talked, unhindered, in her Texas drawl, through wire-clenched teeth.

Alice and Dale's daughter Dusty has cerebral palsy and is severely handicapped. Three years after Dusty was born, their son Darren Russell was born a completely healthy, active little boy. As the years passed, children came over and ran off to play with Darren, leaving Dusty wishing for a friend.

"I started praying and asking God to send Dusty a friend or provide somebody that Dusty could bond with," said Alice. One day the bus driver for Dusty's special preschool told Alice about a fellow little passenger named Kathy, who has spina bifida and is paralyzed from the chest down. Her father, the sole caregiver, was going overseas and needed a home for Kathy for three years. Alice and Dale welcomed Kathy into their home like a child of their own and saw her as a unique blessing. As Alice says, "I'm so pleased that we found a friend for Dusty."

Alice viewed their home, and the love in it, as a gift she would readily give in exchange for the joy and normalcy of a friend for Dusty.

Beauty, Comfort, and Favorite Things

When we think of beautiful homes that we've entered and moved through, they are generally homes of grand scale. We're impressed with big and beautiful. But one of the most beautiful homes I've experienced is very, very small. Small and bare, in fact.

Like all the other houses in this house's neighborhood in Papua New Guinea, it is perched on stilts, about three feet off the sodden ground. As a missionary friend and I entered the makeshift wooden structure we left our shoes at the door, as is the custom. It's becoming the custom in American suburbia too, but somehow in this house I felt a reverence when I slipped off my shoes.

The house was one room, with a kitchen annex that had an open back wall. The only furniture on the wood slat floor was wooden benches placed in a circle for this Bible-study gathering. At night the benches would be pushed against the wall so the family could unroll their sleeping mats. A picture from an outdated calendar decorated the wall. Through the windows and open doors, the jungle blazed green. It was very hot.

When we had completed our study, our Indonesian hostess disappeared into the kitchen area and reappeared with a tray of donuts and something like green pancakes (I didn't ask) filled with grated coconut and brown sugar. Next the tray was brought with sweetened tea in pretty little matching glasses—the kind that Welch's jelly used to come in. I know because my grandmother had these glasses.

It was all served so graciously. And the camera in my heart snapped a memory of simple beauty, of a woman generously sharing the very best she had.

Beauty of Different Sorts

Beauty like this is unexpected. Like classical music, it springs from a combination of balance and surprise. The sense of balance lends peace and rightness and puts us wonderfully at ease. The dash of surprise raises the pulse a bit and triggers a sense of awe. Beauty is a gift! Beauty reminds us that we are created in the image of a creative God who gave us surprising beauty in sunsets and music. We want beauty to surround us in our homes so that we can indulge in beauty in regular doses.

Of course beauty comes in different forms. Some homes wear a "be careful, don't touch, use your best manners" beauty that I find discomforting. I dated a boy whose parents used plastic covers on the furniture in their living room. It always made me feel like they were protecting their furniture from me, so I didn't really want to sit down.

My mother's friend didn't like to have her bridge club at her home because the card table made indentations in her carpet. This is brittle beauty. Homes that are beautiful like this keep you at a distance—feeling like my friend Terri at the art museum. At a special exhibit she stood up very close to a painting to scrutinize it, but when a guard appeared by her elbow, the painting suddenly lost its appeal.

But the beauty of the home where we feel welcome is very different. It conveys a thoughtfulness of comfort and a sense of the personality and character of the people who live within it.

Beauty in our homes reflects our creative best. And it's for our families, not just for our guests.

Developing Your Decorating Style

What is beautiful to you? What is your style? Do you like to have things around you that are traditional or contemporary or southwestern? Maybe you're not sure.

I have fun studying new decorating ideas. I love to settle into my big red chair, put my feet up on the ottoman, and peruse one of my two favorite magazines. I walk into the pictures down a garden path, float on my back in a pool overlooking the ocean, and imagine myself cooking at a kitchen island. Along the way I turn down the corner on favorite pictures or tips. Then, when I've finished reading, I rip out the marked pages for my decorating notebook. It's true that I rarely actually put an idea into practice, but the gorgeous photography and creativity feed my soul and subconsciously sharpen my own sense of personal taste or style.

Let's say that you've been doing your own magazine reading—or you've been watching HGTV, or visiting model homes, or looking at decorating books from the library. You have a pretty good sense of what you like and probably some pictures and particulars in mind. You have dollars in hand (more about dollars later) and are serious about doing some decorating. Where to start? Interior designers, like my friends Vickie and Sharman, will tell you to start with one room at a time. Sure, you want that room to fit into a larger overall plan. But the scope of the task can so easily bog you down. So start with a project that seems manageable, like a room.

First, list all of the functions that will need to happen in that room, suggests Vickie. Let's say it's the family room, and in that room you'll want to watch movies, read a mystery, watch Dad play Pretty Princess board games with the girls, and have snacks with company. You'll need to have seating for six adults. Twenty would be wonderful, but the size of the room says six.

You now know that you'll need a sofa, a table with four chairs, a good lamp for the reading and game-playing, someplace to store some books and board games, and a TV stand or entertainment center.

In placing the furniture, Vickie says, choose a focal point such as a fireplace or the television. Place your largest piece of furniture opposite the focal point to balance the room. Then fill in with the smaller pieces. If you have more than one focal point (perhaps a fireplace and TV), angle the sofa so you can see both.

Now what are you going to do with the walls? Have fun with them! "Paint is the least expensive way to make a big difference in a room," says Sharman, "so don't be afraid to experiment with color. No white walls!"

The one precaution Sharman gives is that if you use too many different colors in different rooms, the result can be a smaller, more chopped-up feel. Designers say it's best if colors flow together and the house has continuity—for example, the same color ceiling and trim throughout all the rooms, or the same color carpet throughout the house, or at least on any one level.

"There are dozens of neutral colors that will warm up a room," adds Vickie, "that go with lots of colors of upholstery and make wood furniture look richer. Light tan or brown, for example, or a caramelly tone will go with most any furniture."

Carpeting should be neutral—neither too light nor too dark. "Think of it as the earth under your feet," says Sharman.

A solid-colored sofa can be a smart choice because sofas are expensive and you'll want to be able to live with it for a long time and change the decor around it and on it. Throws and pillows not only are comfortable, inviting, and cozy but also can add color, pattern, and interest—and can be changed out when you grow tired of them.

Pillows and such fall within a supremely important category, the category that will make the difference in the feel of "house" versus "home." And that category is accessories. Geegaws. Whatnots. The stuff you place around because it makes you happy and brings good memories.

My mother's zany friend Rosie had the only bathroom that I've ever found so memorable that I think about it years after I visited it. Covering the wall of this small half bath were framed cartoons and "blooper" family photos, photos of old movie stars, and jokes and drawings. That room was hard to leave.

The great thing about accessories—not the kind you see in magazine pictures but your own things that you love—is that they can be a bit odd. It just makes them more interesting, because people want to know their story.

In our living room we have two cloud babies suspended from the cathedral ceiling. These are ceramic babies on cottonball "clouds." One of them was a wedding gift (really!), and I don't recall where we got the other one. One has lost her cotton cloud over the years, and the other cloud is graying with dust and age. Frankly, I often forget they're there, except that occasionally when we have guests I'll notice one and wonder if the guests are wondering why in the world cloud babies are flying from the ceiling. So one evening recently I called the whole family into the living room and asked, "Isn't it time to take down the cloud babies?"

The kids, who are all twentysomethings, acted like it was a silly question. Of course we had to keep the cloud babies! That's who we are . . . a family with odd cloud babies suspended in the living room.

Please don't get the wrong idea. I like our rooms to look lovely and balanced and "put together." I try to remember that items are more interesting grouped in threes or in odd numbers and that, as Vickie the designer says, items are more interesting when you work with opposites: something shiny with something dull, some-

RAISING A GOOD FAMILY DOG

When dogs are home mates, we want them to be less a nuisance and more a "favorite thing." We want them to play catch with a Frisbee and curl up by the fireplace on a winter's day. Dr. David Chubb of the Perfect Puppy Academy in Santa Barbara, California, has these tips for success in raising a puppy to be a good family companion:

Puppies have a crucial socialization period at eight to fourteen weeks old. During those weeks the puppy should have positive relationships with as many different people, dogs, and environments as possible. Most behavior problems develop because a dog isn't well socialized when young.

If you choose an older dog from a private owner or rescue or shelter, be sure that you are able to get good information on the dog's personality and traits. In other words, be sure the previous owner has worked with and studied the dog.

If you purchase a dog from a breeder, be sure the dog has been bred as a house pet. The dog should have spent some of his earliest weeks in a home with a family instead of just in a cage.

When choosing a breed, keep in mind that some breeds require more maintenance and attention than others. The herding breeds, like Australian shepherds and border collies, are always thinking and need to be working, using their brains and bodies all the time. You can't just stick them in a house or yard—they will think up mischief. Guard dogs, like German shepherds and rottweilers particularly, must have lots of socialization

thing tall with something short, something soft with something hard. And nothing adds soothing softness quite like (healthy) green plants. I do work at all that, particularly in my two pretty rooms. But a few quirky, surprising things can also add fun.

In our home the two pretty rooms are the living room/dining room and the master bedroom. They are the only two rooms that are truly "decorated" and for which we bought new furniture when we moved into this home. No matter what the other rooms of the house look like at any given time, I try to keep these two rooms picked up and the bed in the bedroom made because then I know there are two safe oases: one for taking a visitor and the other for just spending some peaceful moments.

when they're young. Most of the little breeds, if bred correctly, can be very good house pets. Labrador retrievers are by far the most popular breed of dog, but they can be very boisterous and difficult for a young child to handle.

Pairing a puppy and a young child is a challenge, because puppies are children too. Because of the way a young child moves, a puppy will think the child is a playmate and will nip, jump, lunge, and bark at him. The puppy is just doing what's appropriate for puppies.

Children should do some hand feeding of your pet. This helps establish the child as one of the dog's leaders. It says, "Look, I have your most important resource." Let the child feed the dog kibble piece by piece as the dog responds to some basic commands like sitting and lying down.

When a child approaches a dog, she should stop and allow the dog to come to her, and then put out her hand lower than the dog's head, palm out. Putting the hand down on the dog's head can be seen as aggression by the dog. Watch for any signs that the dog is uncomfortable. If the dog is backing off or afraid, stay away from the dog. And if the dog is playing too rough, separate from the dog.

Favorite Things

Homes are places to preserve and enjoy one's favorite things. Unfortunately, sometimes Alex's favorite things are *not* my favorite things and vice versa.

The first argument of our married life developed over the decorating of our apartment. It wasn't just that I didn't like the beads he wanted to hang in the doorway or the cheap mountain-scene painting he had "doctored up" with random touches of acrylic paint and hung over the sofa. That was bad enough—I had to live here! The real problem was that I had taken it for granted that I would decorate the place and he would arrange tools in the garage or something. He was not only invading my territory, he was setting up camp!

When tastes collide, sometimes you just have to figure out which of you it matters to most. If it matters to me more, then maybe Alex will give. But next time, or when it matters to him more, I have to be ready to compromise too.

Take Alex's water feature in the backyard. This definitely fits into the category of his favorite things. Adjacent to our patio we have a berm landscaped in delicate, purple-flowered vinca and other perennial ground covers and shaded by a candlestick pine, an aspen, and another small, shapely tree. Water tumbles gracefully through three tiers of small pools. On summer evenings Alex pulls over a lawn chair and sits by his water feature in the shade. He really does love it.

Over the years he's tried to improve it. He added goldfish, but within a day the birds had consumed them. He replaced the filter several times after the dog chewed on it. He resurfaced the pools. But one time he decided to add onto the water feature and—without a plan and without talking to me about it—started hacking into "my" vinca. Well! Let's just say that we have since established boundaries between the vinca and the water feature. We try to respect each other's favorite things.

Our favorite things can also serve as underpinnings. They tie us to good memories and often to past generations. They give us a sense of legacy, or continuity, or being in the flow of something greater than we are as individuals. My favorite things include a round, covered, silver serving dish with a removable enamel dish inside that belonged to my mother's mother. Engraved on the lid is a large calligraphic "H." This stands for Hawley, which was my great-grandmother's married name. I marvel at how old this could be. When I polish it, when I dish in the food, and when I then put it on the table, offering its contents to loved ones for Christmas dinner or on Easter, I am connected to women in my family who watched covered wagons roll past their little Kansas town, heading west. I can buy lovely, practical things at Crate and Barrel, but I can't buy that richness! At the same time, I can take good care of a few new things I enjoy that may (who knows?) be treasured in turn by future generations.

Another of my favorite things is a tiny framed photograph of my father at about age sixteen, in overalls, working on a motor, on the farm in Kansas where he grew up. Here is what I love about this photo: My father died when I was twenty-four, before my three sons were born. So to my boys my father is a blank; they have no memory of him. However, the handsome, confident, smiling face in this photo is so, so, *so* like my oldest son Tim at the same age, just with different coloring. And get this—Tim also loves tinkering with bicycles and mechanical things. So this tiny photo affirms in my heart the connectedness of generations, the flow-through of genes that involves not only appearance but also competencies. What a treasure!

We each have a few things, often photographs, that are especially worth protecting (including from unsupervised little hands), displaying, using, and enjoying.

Buying, Comparing, and Sharing

Decorating and furnishing our homes and buying accessories is so fun and rewarding, and also pretty easy to justify: it's not just for us, after all, but for family members to enjoy too. It dips into a deeply creative nesting place in our souls.

It can also take us into the dangerous territory of comparing our home with the homes of our friends and our neighbors. Some people seem to have unlimited dollars with which to decorate and fill their homes. A combination of envy of that ability and a pride that wants our home to also look good easily lures us into overspending. I've been there.

I can almost guarantee that you know people whose homes are larger and more beautiful than yours, and you know people whose homes are smaller and less beautiful. Your whole life it will be this way. It doesn't matter where yours fits in the spectrum. It really doesn't.

Our standard of living, the things we think we *have* to provide for our families—from the latest electronics to gymnastics classes—is precariously driven by what the families around us are providing. Sometimes it is actually *better* to provide our children less of what can be bought and more of our time and more need to use their imaginations. Our son Dan will recount happy memories of setting up little plastic army men in the sandbox with his friend Larry and then flooding it, but he won't tell you about the hours he spent playing video games.

Anne, one of my closest friends, is an interior designer. This is both a negative and a positive: she does not hesitate to critique my decor, but she also helps me with it. The fact that her house is always gorgeous *and current* is also both good and bad. Frankly, it makes me want to make lots of changes in my home, but I also enjoy being in hers. What we do for each other that is entirely positive is that we share. One time Anne and a fellow designer shared their talent with me. They came to my house and we went room by room rearranging furniture, accessories, and the pictures on the walls. When they left I had a house that looked great, and I hadn't spent a dime. When Anne has a party, I loan her my patio tablecloths. I loan her my flatware, the punchbowl and cups that we own jointly (and she likes me to store), and whatever else I have to contribute. She in turn does the same for me. We will always have the tendency to compare. But Anne and I have learned to look that urge in the eyes for what it is and choose to enjoy and share with each other instead.

Another land mine of decorating is that spending money can make us feel good. In *Blue Like Jazz*, author Donald Miller talks about the fact that he has a problem with buying things that he doesn't really need, and he explains it this way: "I saw this documentary about the brain that says habits are formed when the 'pleasure center' of the brain lights up as we do a certain behavior. The documentary said that some people's pleasure centers light up when they buy things. I wondered if my pleasure center did that."[1] Does your pleasure center light up when you buy things for your home? Mine does. I just have to make sure I am not spending too much time indulging that pleasure center. Debt can be mentally and emotionally (to say nothing of maritally) debilitating, and the stress is not erased by lounging in a beautifully decorated room. One thing that I've learned helps me is to stay out of the stores if I can't afford to buy. What you don't see won't hurt you!

Contentment

Contentment is a precious quality, one that oozes out of you to salve those around you. It is a strong antidote to comparison. And it comes more easily than you might think if you search through your life for all the things for which you're thankful, if you count your blessings and rehearse them in your mind. Contentment is important not only for the person with a not-so-great-seeming home. I have observed that people with gorgeous homes that most people would envy are still not content with them. Perhaps it's due to boredom, but something is always not quite right. How sad! I hope you're enjoying the home that is yours right now without longing for a different home to be yours tomorrow.

The blessing of a home—particularly a spacious, attractive home—is a responsibility, a stewardship. This is just a principle of life: we enjoy our things more when we're willing to share them with others.

I know a couple who live in what most would call a mansion. It is a historic home that they have lovingly restored from its interim life when it was chopped up into offices. Its acre of stately grounds is canopied by towering oak trees that protectively hedge the house from the city around it. Each year just before Easter, this couple hosts on their lawn an Easter egg hunt for children who are confined to wheelchairs. The entire event is planned with the delight and the capabilities of these children in mind. The couple marvels at the way the children help each other. It is a very happy day. In a way this home must be happy too. Beautiful homes are to be enjoyed and shared, no matter how big or how small.

Home Tour: Let's Be Comfortable

Kathy G. makes comfort the key criteria for her home. "To me, beauty and comfort have to go hand in hand," she says. "I like every room in our home to be comfortable. I decorate around that, and it will be beautiful."

So when she and her husband Tom shop for a chair, they sit in it. They consider whether it will be comfortable if they're going to watch a movie in it.

Several of the beautiful, comfortable, and favorite things in Kathy and Tom's home have come from the hobbies of Kathy's parents. Kathy's mother sewed each grandchild comforters that have come to be known as "Grandma Blankies." These comforters are all made of a fabric sheet on one side, widths of fabric on the other, and batting in the middle. Occasional yarns anchor the layers. Grandma Blankies go on picnics, go camping, are cuddled under for movies, and are thrown into the washing machine. The nearly grown kids show no sign of outgrowing them. Kathy's father enjoys woodworking, so he's crafted cedar chests for his granddaughters and a coffee table with a compartment for each grandson.

"My philosophy is if I surround myself with the things I love, then I'll love my home," says Kathy. In the living room an antique clock that has been in her family for over a hundred years shares a shelf with a ceramic house that her son Adam made in the sixth grade.

The main wall in the dining room displays a collection of Twelve Days of Christmas blue and white china plates. The collection was begun by Tom's mother when Tom was twelve years old, and his mother gave them to Kathy and Tom as a wedding gift. They are not in a hutch or stored in the basement until Christmas but displayed on the wall. Kathy has decorated the rest of the room, including the choice of paint color for the wall, around these special plates.

Lighting is one way Kathy intentionally makes their home warm and cozy. She uses strategically placed candles because she loves the warmth of the glow. Two small decorative lamps in corners of the kitchen make this a happy place to visit in the night. She turns them on each evening as the sun goes down.

Tom uses halogen bulbs in floor-standing canisters to create soft lighting in strategic places like the top of the TV armoire, in the corner behind an easy chair or ficus tree, and above the closets in rooms with vaulted ceilings. The result is soft lighting that gives the rooms a warm feeling without the harsh glare of overhead lights.

Home Tour: Shari's Style

Shari's living room is a rich plum color on the walls and in the furnishings. It's a small room but not cluttered, and as your eye travels around it, she describes the story or significance of each piece: "That's Dave's grandmother's oriental rug on the floor. These chairs of his grandfather's we recovered. The lamp behind you I got at a thrift sale. I've started that collection of little molds on the mantel. The frog pitcher? I just like him. I got the prints at an antique store. They were in really bad frames and I had them redone."

Shari's design philosophy is to buy the best stuff she can. She looks carefully at thrift stores and garage sales to find a sofa or chairs that are of high structural quality and so worth recovering. She doesn't feel the need to change the decor often except perhaps a few accessories. "I know what I like," she says, smiling. "I don't have to have someone tell me every two years I have to change it."

Shari wants her home to look like and be a place that is safe, where you can explore, and where you'll be loved, surrounded, laughed with, and taken seriously. "I don't want my home to be too poofy," Shari says, "because that says 'don't take me seriously.' I want it to have a sense of humor, because life is a process to laugh at and jump in and be surrounded by, because it's hard.

"Building a home is a process, just like life," says Shari. "You can tell when someone's come in and put everything in at one time and it's fresh and clean and new, and there's something that lacks interest to me, as opposed to someone who has built this home and added pieces that reflect them over time."

My Space, Our Space, and Creativity

A trail high in the Rockies climbs through lodgepole pines, blue spruce, and aspen and then opens into a broad meadow. In this high valley the wind ripples tall grasses in soft waves. Through the center of the meadow meanders a stream clear enough to show the rocks on the bottom, even through the deep, fast water midstream.

The trail continues, skirting the edge of the woods but continually in view of the meadow. Every time I hike this trail, I'm so captivated with the meadow vista that coming upon the ruin of a lone homestead cabin takes me by surprise. The cabin is made of logs stacked like Lincoln Logs and chinked with newspapers and mud. Of course, each time I hike by I scour the debris for bits of newspaper, but it has all disintegrated or has been taken by other hikers as souvenirs.

When I duck to pass through the doorway, I feel like an intruder in a family's dwelling of more than a hundred years ago. The roof has caved in so that the floor is a jumble of weeds and timbers. Two windows flank the door, framing the meadow and giving the home a deep, clean breath in a dark, enclosing forest.

The whole cabin is about the size of an average kitchen, and I try to imagine a family, with more than 2.3 children, contained hour by hour in that room and sleeping in little beds in a loft or bunched together in a couple of bigger beds.

Did this family feel confined? Trapped? Stifled? Surely in the winter they must have. Especially the mother if the father left to trap game or work a mine. How did they adapt to their space, making it meet their private needs as well as their needs for the company of one another in the midst of the wild elements outside the windows?

It reminds me of the *Little House on the Prairie* stories, where the Ingalls family sat around the stove at night, Ma and the girls sewing and Pa playing his fiddle. Were they so in tune with each other that close quarters didn't matter? Or did they each take extended visits to the privy?

We've come a long way from confined cabin living. Most of us Americans look for the biggest space our income will allow when we're raising families. Bigger is considered better!

But bigger can also be echoey and impersonal. Sometimes smaller is better. Smaller can be cozy in ways that bigger can't. We all need some cozy, even if it's in a corner of a big space.

Creating Coziness

Hiding in a small space is something most of us need to do on a regular basis. Personally, my whole life as a mother I've needed to start the day sitting in bed, propped on two pillows, with a cup of coffee, a piece of toast with jelly, my planner, my Bible—and no one talking to me. If I don't get that time, I'm some degree of cranky for the rest of the day because I'm off balance.

A small space of one's own provides a buffer from the demands of larger life and larger space. Jill's family had to relinquish a suburban home for transitional housing in a converted motel room, and the main thing she missed was the ability to separate her three kids from one another and herself from them. In their house the kids could go to the basement or outside or to the upstairs loft. They had different places to go for their own space and time.

In their new temporary setting, Jill recognized that just changing their sleeping arrangement would allow each of them a perimeter of their own space. She had one of the two queen-size beds hauled out of their all-purpose room and three twin beds hauled in, two of them bunked. Now the three children each have a bit of their own territory. "When you go to bed at night, it's your space," said Jill. From the storage unit that holds all their belongings, Jill scrounged all their own pillows, pillowcases, throw blankets, and stuffed animals. These added the comfort of something that was theirs to enjoy in their own space.

Of course Jill and her family also still have the universal home refuge—the bathroom. It's the one room where you can lock yourself in, and all others out, with no need for explanations. Chrissy, a single mom, has created of her master bathroom the ultimate magazine take-me-away ad. Walls faux painted Caribbean blue envelop her with ocean. Seashells hot-glued in place frame her mirror, a palm tree "sways" in the corner, and a small TV perches opposite the tub. After her kids are asleep, Chrissy indulges in a bubble bath, a glass of wine, and a chick flick in a tropical paradise.

Cozy spaces tend to be safe, private, soft, and not too bright. Often they are places where we, like Chrissy in her bathroom, have staked a claim in recognition of our needs and created a refuge.

In a scene from the book *Plainsong*, two old bachelor ranchers have taken in a homeless pregnant teenager. She disappears into "her" room after dinner, and they wonder what she is doing:

> When he had both boots oiled to his requirements Harold stood up and set them out in the kitchen where they gleamed mutely against the wall. Then he came back and crossed to her door and stood listening with his head canted and his eyes staring. He knocked on the door.

Victoria? He said.

Yes.

Everything all right in there?

You can come in, she said.

So he entered her room. It was hers already. She had made it so. It was female now, cleaner and tidier, with little things set out in place. For the first time in half a century someone had taken an interest in the room. The old cardboard boxes were pushed under the bed and the clothes in the closet had been shoved back farther into the dark. Against the wall the old mahogany chest of drawers, its oval mirror darkened and finely cracked at the edges, had been dusted and polished, and her belongings were now arranged on it, hair ribbons and comb and brush, lipstick and liner, hair clasps, a little cedar box of jewelry whose lid was closed by a tiny brass lock.

She herself was sitting up in the bed in a square-necked winter nightgown with a sweater pulled over her shoulders, a schoolbook and a blue notepad propped up in her lap, while the lamp beside the bed cast yellow light onto her clear face and her shining dark hair.

I just was wondering, he said. If you was warm enough in here.

Yes, she said. It's fine.

They're saying how it's suppose to get kind of cold tonight. Is it?

And this old house ain't very warm.

I'm fine, she said again. She watched him. He was standing just inside the door, his hands poked into his pockets, his weather-blasted red face shining in the lamplight.

Anyhow, he said. He peered around. You think of something, you can let us know. We don't know much about this sort of thing.

Thank you, she said.

He looked at her once more, quickly, as some shy country animal might, and closed the door. [1]

Victoria arranged her own cozy space, a buffer for her life with two old bachelor farmers.

Private Space

When siblings or roommates share a room, there are small ways and big ways to create private space for each person.

Jennifer's two sons share a bedroom and an age difference of seven years. To help the boys sense that their room reflects both of their personalities, Jennifer asked an artist friend to paint murals on the walls and let the boys choose what the art would be. On the largest wall a cowboy with lasso twirling 'round his head straddles a rearing horse. Another wall pictures mountains, a sunset, and peacefully grazing cattle. A turtle and a lizard creep by one of the boys' beds. By the door are painted cowboy boots in two sizes.

Brandy's daughters, ages six and eight, share a room that is painted a different color on each girl's side. A large wooden wardrobe separates the girls' spaces, giving a sense of partition to the room.

Another way to approach room sharing is by creating a larger-than-both-of-them sense of space. While my brother lived with us for a few months, he surprised Dan and Drew, who shared a bedroom, by stenciling constellations on their bedroom ceiling in glow-in-the-dark paint. Then as they looked at the ceiling at night, they could be as far away—and as far away from their brother—as they dreamt to be.

Kids also find enclosed "hiding" spaces secure and comforting. A popular spot at Lindsey's daughter's preschool is a cozy loft that is furnished underneath with books, a child-sized recliner, and a tape recorder for listening to stories.

Sharing Cozy Spaces

I remember how as a child I loved the dark, cool oasis of my parents' bedroom in our old two-story house in Topeka, since it and the living room had the only window air conditioners.

The other dominant feature in the room was their twin beds, separated by a table with a reading lamp. I suppose that I assumed everybody's mom and dad slept in twin beds. Of course eventually I learned about that.

Now the American couple's bed has stretched from twins or at most a full-size bed (imagine—they thought that was full-size) to a queen or often a king. And with that stretch lots of monkeys are now if not actually jumping on the bed, at least hanging out in it.

Liz, who has four young children, says of their family bed, "We watch TV there a lot, or we just snuggle. In the morning they all pile in, so there's six of us in the bed together. I love those times. Sweet, sweet times, when they're still all in their pj's. And when Dad's gone, we eat popcorn in bed!"

George Howe Colt, author of *The Big House*, writes eloquently of his family's "Big Bed":

> The Big Bed was the blank slate on which the story of our family was inscribed. It's where the children opened their stockings on Christmas morning; it's where we had breakfast on Mother's Day. It's where, on special occasions, we had their "lie-bys," a bedtime ritual Anne had inherited from her own childhood, during which we'd sing lullabies and talk with them about their days. It's where we tended our children's strep throat, where Anne recovered from bronchitis, and where I lay for six weeks with an injured back, reading James Fenimore Cooper. It's where Henry retreated when his feelings were hurt, where Susannah wept when her goldfish died, where Anne surrounded herself with pillows after the death of her father. It's where Anne and I rendezvoused when we needed to talk. "Meet me on the Big Bed," we would say. . . . And it was where, each morning, we'd hear the door open and the sound of footsteps padding across the floor, before the children crawled into bed with us and, with any luck, fell back to sleep.[2]

What if the kids aren't so young? Our boys have always joined us to talk, and now, as young men, they think nothing of knocking and coming in, even if no sliver of light still shows in the crack between carpet and bedroom door. Drew, who is built like a tank, dives across the foot of the bed, which crackles and groans. And remember that I said this is one of our two pretty rooms with good-quality furniture, so it's really quite distressing. Our daughter-in-law is emboldened by the fact that the others come right in, so she does too.

They'll talk to us in the dark or in the cozy glow of a reading lamp. Voices are soft and the subjects closer to the heart in the dark.

Sometimes, of course, the voices in the dark need to be limited to two, because Mom and Dad need special intimate times in their bedroom too, when the kids have said "goodnight to the stars, the air, goodnight to voices everywhere"[3] from their own beds.

Connecting Places

Even in our home's larger areas, where we hang out with family or friends, we like to create intimate, grouped-together spaces. Tammy and her kids like to play games together in their family room. "We sit on the floor. The ceiling is lower. It feels cozy. We play UNO Attack, and Sorry. My husband and I like to play cribbage."

For Sherry that cozy space is her kitchen. She sees her kitchen as a "bridge" or place to start building relationships with family or people they've invited over. "I love it being big, bright," she says. "You can sit on the island, you can sit at the table. It's a central place of fellowship for me and my family."

You may be thinking, *But my family doesn't seem to care about spending time together—really together—in a cozy space.* What then? Rick McKinley writes, "When you grow up in a home where individuals are doing little more than sharing space, you miss out on key relationships that create a sense of security and belonging. And you're left with a homeless heart."[4] None of us

FIVE TOOLS FOR THE HOME

Pastor Don Marxhausen has performed countless weddings. He's good at it, if he does say so himself, because he gives these five tools in the ceremony. Actually he's not sure how much the marrying couples absorb, but he's confident that the already-married audience is listening. These apply well as rules for a home, ones that make it a more peaceful place.

Say "I'm sorry." It's important not that you be right but that you be in relationship. Admit when you've been wrong—or if you've been right with an overbearing attitude.

Say "please." Women expect a man to know what they're feeling. Men expect a woman to know what they're thinking. Neither is the case. Let the other person know what you need.

Remember. People tend to forget. Recall the past in such a way that it's brought to the present and made a strength for the future. On the days you're at your worst, remember the days you were at your best: when you had your first kiss, when you began to dream together, and so on.

Laugh. Laughter is a sign of the Holy Spirit, because you have to surrender in order to laugh. You can't be in control when you laugh.

Express gratitude. The most positive emotion is gratitude. The worst emotion for the human body is revenge; the next worst is hatred; the third worst is anger. But it's amazing how far it goes to say "thank you."

wants a homeless heart—for ourselves or for our loved ones. We must think of ways to reach across our shared spaces.

One way to encourage a family shift in the direction of intimate interactions is with food: comfort foods, favorite foods, preferably ones that have been prepared on the premises so that aromas are part of the experience. Food is huge.

Amy and Heidi are twin twentysomething Australian women who have traveled the world. They've been to Europe, Canada, New York, and Boston, and have driven from Los Angeles to Florida and back. They are not women who pine with homesickness. Yet when you ask them what they miss about home, the words tumble out: "We miss the food. I've already put in my order back home. My favorite Australian baked dinner, a roast. Chicken—breaded—and baked vegetables: sweet potatoes, potatoes, pumpkin. And spinach. . . . Our spinach is different than here. It's very leafy. . . . Chicken nuggets. Spaghetti. Seafood. Christmas we have baked dinner for our lunch then at dinnertime we have seafood." The way to a family's heart is through their stomachs—through their stomachs being thoughtfully provided something that they like. Like ice cream sundaes or popcorn or nachos. Do you know what your family's favorites are? Lindsey posted her family's list inside a cupboard door. (We'll talk more about food in the next chapter.)

The second type of preparation that can help move families toward interaction is relational and requires persistent little steps. It takes being undaunted and willing to change tactics but keep working the plan.

Anne and Glenn had a newly blended family of six children. One visiting daughter, a young teen, had chosen to sunbathe on the patio while the rest of the family ate lunch inside. When her dad called her in, she said, "Why? What's the big deal?" Well, conversation around the table really might be a big deal—a little big deal. Most big deals, after all, are made up of lots of little pieces. Persuading her to come in and participate—to at least drink a glass of iced tea with them—might be worth the hassle.

Giving family members some preparation time (or forewarning) and some degree of choice also helps. Let's say that you see a game night as having positive possibilities. Choose a time—not too much time—and ask the family member most likely to challenge the process to choose what the game will be. After this, choices can be rotated.

Beware of using methods like drawing straws. Rather, the order must be fixed, something like moving in order of birthdays in the year. One summer we drove through Colorado. Nine hours each way in a station wagon with the three boys wedged together in the middle seat. Lots of elbow jabbing and worse, let me tell you.

Of course the window seats were prime, so we decided that each time we stopped, we would draw straws to see who had to sit in the middle for the next segment of the trip. Drew, the youngest, lost the draw every time. *Every single time.* We tried hard to rig the length of the straws and to coax him to the correct choice. Wrong every time. It has scarred him for life.

Give little choices to encourage family interaction, but don't always give freedom to make the big choice "Do I have to do this?" Be persistent. Work the plan.

Margins and Space

Whenever I have been so busy that I feel like I'm landing at home just long enough for pit stops—when those cycles finally end, I love nothing more than to diddle my way through a day at home, getting reacquainted with its special spaces. I miss my home when I'm hyper-busy. I have to mark off time to change out the seasonal decorations and stock up on necessary supplies and open the blinds just so and plop in my favorite red chair with a magazine and remember its comfort.

We must create space in our lives to enjoy the space in our homes. One of Liz's favorite things is to be at home with no one else there, "Because when you have a larger family," she says, "if it's not one child, it's another. They love you and want you, but sometimes it's nice to finish a thought" in your own space.

How does a mother of young children obtain the luxury of being at home alone? One way is by what Charlie, Stephanie R.'s husband, calls Dad-Son-Son-Daughter Saturdays. Charlie takes the three kids to do whatever it is that he wants to do or something he thinks would be fun for the kids. It might be the Sportsman's Show, but they're sure to have fun.

How does Mommy get time at home alone if Daddy's help is

not an option? Trade babysitting with a friend, or sometimes hire a babysitter for the day—one who sits in her own home—and buy yourself time to do whatever you want to do at home.

Lee Ann keeps margins around her four children's activities so that they have time together at home. She says, "I don't push them to do sports. We don't look for sports. My kids don't get a lot of lessons. Nobody ever had piano. I feel like they can always develop skills when they leave, but right now they need family time. My oldest son plays baseball for his school. My next son plays tennis. My daughter is picking up guitar. But unless they choose sports or decide they want to do something [they don't do it]. . . . If they do decide, we will do whatever we can to help them [participate]. [But] I really guard that family time."

Just as the margins on this page have been set to a standard width to make the type comfortable for you to read, so margins in life must be consciously set: some time at home, some time alone, gaps in the busyness, purposeful aimlessness!

Mom in Space

Mom. Her very presence gives substance and security to a home space. This reality surfaced time and again in my interviews for this book. We see this in Chrissy's five-year-old daughter Alexie: "Alexie likes to be anywhere I am. She follows me. If I'm watching TV and folding laundry, she'll help me." And we hear it when Claire tells us, "We have a flat kitchen counter, and when the girls were little, they would do homework or work on projects there with me while I cooked dinner." Older kids? When I asked Chuck what their grown boys look forward to at home, he said, "Their mother. All of them have a connection to their mother. They will communicate more with their mom. We'll say maybe a few sentences. But with her they'll talk and talk and talk."

Obviously mom can't be everywhere all the time. So we must try to find the balance of being physically present while also meeting other needs and responsibilities. And we must try to be attentive when present. It's one of those dynamic tensions that constantly play over a mom's life.

Being Creative at Home

I don't know this for a fact, but I believe that the act of expressing creativity must release those endorphins that runners brag about. I watch my son Dan hunched intently over his stamp collection at his kitchen table, searching through a pile of colored squares for one from the country whose page lies opened as he pursues his goal of collecting a stamp from each country in the United Nations. If only a runner knew that she could accomplish the same rush of well-being with her butt in a chair!

The expression of creativity holds a touch of the divine, a manifestation of the fact that we have been created in the image of a holy God. We are all wired to be creative. And home is a great place to do it.

Defining Creativity

Children ooze creativity naturally and constantly. But somehow as adults we have to talk ourselves into letting ourselves take the time to be creative. Or—amazingly!—we don't think that we are creative. Perhaps it's because we worry about *definitions* of creativity, whereas kids just blissfully are.

I asked a group of moms with young children how they (the moms) expressed creativity at home, and this is what they said:

"I used to be a costume designer, and I have a workroom in the basement. I just go down there and look at my fabrics and fringes and make something. I totally love that and am re-energized."

Liz

"I love to play with my kids almost to the detriment of anything getting done in my house."

Tammy

"I'm not house creative. My greatest creativity is using my spiritual gift that God has given me: I teach."

Sherry

"Because I'm not crafty I think of creativity more as expressing individuality. I try not to pigeonhole my daughter. I try to find what strengths she has and encourage individuality."

Kelly

"Color. I love to see color! I've painted every room in my house a different color: burgundy, hunter green, navy blue."

Chrissy

Rebecca grew up in a small, remote town in northern Alberta, Canada. She didn't have many amenities or enrichment programs available to her. But she took piano lessons, and she started cooking while in early elementary school. "I liked to get into the kitchen and see what would happen," she says. And still, mostly on weekends, Rebecca likes to get into the kitchen and see what happens. Sometimes creativity means working with what we have, even though it's not much. In fact, that's creativity at its best.

The Creative Atmosphere

In a little room off an upstairs bathroom—sort of a builder's oops of a room—Stephanie keeps a long church-potluck-type table for her gift wrap and her scrapbooking supplies. All this is actually stored under the table hidden by a tablecloth—her hidden treasures. More than anything Stephanie R. loves to work on her scrapbooks. She says she cries half the time she does, "from the sweetness of the memories." Her kids love to pour over them. Charlie, her husband, loves them too; he'll say, "Oh, Stephanie, this is great. Good job! Thanks for doing these." What a recipe for creative success!

An encouraging environment is such a boost to the joy of expressing creativity. We all love attention and applause. And the reverse is also true: if the fruit of our creativity is constantly judged and compared and criticized, if we're prodded to stay within the lines, the lid to all those creative juices goes on tight. Creative expression requires freedom and encouragement to thrive.

Lee Ann's friend was tearing down a wall in her house, so she let people write whatever they wanted on it before the wall came down. "I thought it would be fun to keep a wall like that," says Lee Ann. So now one wall of her kitchen is fair game for a guest to sign and date it and write why they were there. One neighbor put his bare foot against the wall as far up as he could reach it, traced it, and then wrote in the foot. "People love it," says Lee Ann. "They feel like they're breaking a rule when they write on the wall. Sometimes they'll draw a picture or write a poem."

Adam's creativity soared around his Lego constructions, and his mom Kathy G. saw a way to encourage his creativity while expressing her own. Covering one wall of Adam's bedroom, Kathy painted scenes to match his different Lego collections. In the center a mountain was topped by a dark sky studded with stars. Using cheap balsa wood shelves that Kathy assembled and screwed into the wall, Adam displayed Lego skiers schussing the mountain and spaceships traversing the sky. At the base of the mountain a beach, complete with palm trees and lapping ocean waves, held shelves for Lego jet runners. A desert scene with Lego Star Wars constructions and a cityscape with shelves for ambulances and police cars flanked the sides of the mountain. Adam built up his collections at each birthday and played Legos by the hour alone or with friends. "Paint is so cheap," says Kathy. "For this purpose you could even use acrylics." And of course it could be painted over when Adam's Lego mania played out.

Do We Keep All This Creative Stuff?

How do we decide what creative treasures to keep and what to, well, not keep? Children are creative every day. We want to encourage them on the one hand and not drown in paper on the other.

Digital photos are a terrific way to preserve a wealth of their creations. But a few of them you've just got to be able to handle, you know? Our basement storage room houses one storage bin for each of our three sons, each holding the best of the best artwork and stories from their preschool and elementary school years. I whittled down the collection year by year and then let them help me make the final selections for the bins. A few of their pictures that were most expressive of the personalities of the artists I've framed for my home office wall.

The hard part will come when I must decide whether these bins stay tucked away in our home or will be transferred to their own. When the time comes, I think I'll enjoy going through the bins and giving selectively—returning the bins safely to their places at our house.

As adults what do we keep of our own creative outpourings? My mother and her friends went through a phase where they crocheted bracelets with stretchy gold yarn and gold buttons of different shapes and sizes. I loved stretching the bracelet and twisting my wrist to admire it. The phase passed and the bracelet passed too, but I wish I had it today. I wish that my mother had kept her button bracelet. How was she to know?

I think we should keep those things we've taken particular pride in creating—no matter whether anyone else enjoys them or not. And I think we should also keep things we've created that seem to be particularly fascinating to a child. I wish my mom had noticed that I sure liked that button bracelet.

The Right Space

Among the highest and best functions of our home spaces is providing niches where we can let down and be alone, places conducive to connecting and being cozy together, and the right spaces and resources to exercise the joy of creativity.

Home Tour: Creativity in an Urban Space

Rebecca and Nathan love the sense of history that pervades their loft apartment downtown. They like the fact that it's old and so understandably rough around the edges. It was built in the 1890s, probably by Pittsburgh Plate Glass (which is why the windows are so large). A neighbor found a turn-of-the century photo of the building at the library and shared it with the apartment community.

Rebecca and Nathan have also lived in the suburbs, and she sees suburban communities in comparison to urban as managed creativity. Even though creativity is involved in building any new house, in the suburbs, she says, it's as if you are being creative within an assigned palate.

Rebecca feels like in the city the palate is much larger. You can be eclectic. Pointing out objects around the apartment, she explains: "Over there is a very square, metal, boxy, modern table. But the dining table we're sitting at was made from old wood planks from Indiana. There's just something about having a range of materials to work with . . . whatever strikes your fancy fits."

As Rebecca points out, they have no framed family photos around the room. Her favorite things are mementoes rather than photos. "I enjoy the metaphor of the object," she says. So a chalkboard reminds her of the friend down the street who gave it to her as a child. A painting speaks of the friend who created it.

The couple loves the fact that it's an environment they both like—and they chose it together. They have never lived anywhere for longer than six years. Who knows how long they'll stay? But for the moment it is home. And they like it.

Home Tour: Creating Cozy Zones

A cozy place can be a zone created in a large space. The first floor of Ginger's hundred-year-old home is one long, open, high-ceilinged room. Using area rugs and furniture groupings for definition, she's created a comfortable space to sit and visit or watch TV at the front end of the room. She stores the TV in a closed wooden cabinet across from the cushy sofa so that it doesn't dominate the whole space.

At the other end of the room the dining table and chairs are separated from the kitchen by a large, curved breakfast bar. It creates a warm, informal area for guests or family to gab or work on a project while Ginger or her husband cooks.

The third area includes a built-in desk/work station that's on the back wall of the house in a corner of the kitchen. A small window above the desk overlooks the backyard. Sometimes a glimpse of growing things outside is enough to create a private-feeling space, as is the case here. The overall result is that one long room feels like three different spaces as well as one.

Dining In

When I opened the front door one afternoon to find eight-year-old Joseph on the porch, I recognized him as the new boy who had moved in up the street. He had seen Drew playing in our yard and came over to make a new friend.

But I don't recall that Joseph ever made it up to Drew's room to play. Instead he followed me, or rather followed his nose, to the kitchen, where I was baking chocolate chip cookies. In those days, when I was a home-based mom, it was as if I had read "Thou shalt bake lots and lots and lots of chocolate chip cookies" in the Good Mommy Manual. All of our family members now sport a good ten pounds that could be attributed to chocolate chip cookies constantly filling the jar.

"Are you the grandma?" Joseph asked me. Was this the thanks I got for my gift to him of a perfect, flexibly warm chocolate chip cookie? I decided that it must be the apron. I have routinely worn an apron in the kitchen since my pregnancy days, when I seemed to always have a moist line on my shirt where my tummy met the counter. It's also handy for catching jumping red spaghetti sauce. Aprons keep me from feeling nervous in the kitchen.

Before I could set the record straight, Joseph continued in a rush. "My grandma [his stepmother's mother] bakes chocolate chip cookies too, and I get to help her. I didn't get to go to kindergarten because my real mommy stole me and she hid me in her house and I couldn't go out so I didn't go to kindergarten, but now I get to bake chocolate chip cookies with my grandma."

I certainly had learned a lot about Joseph!

I don't think it's possible to overestimate the power of the connection between good home-cooked food with good aromas and security, comfort, and well-being.

On any given night we're preoccupied with figuring out how, where, and what everyone will eat, intent on getting the meal accomplished in the context of the family's schedule. We're juggling soccer practice and an evening class, Dad's being out of town and the need to go to the grocery store for two items. But if we can finally get to the table, just look at what is actually happening night by night behind the scenes:

> [Research that has been accumulating from very disparate fields] shows how eating ordinary, average everyday supper with your family is strongly linked to lower incidence of bad outcomes such as teenage drug and alcohol use, and to good qualities like emotional stability. It correlates with kindergarteners being better prepared to learn to read. (It even trumps getting read to.) Regular family supper helps keep asthmatic kids out of hospitals. It discourages both obesity and eating disorders. It supports your staying more connected to your extended family, your ethnic heritage, your community of faith. It will help children and families to be more resilient, reacting positively to those curves and arrows that life throws our way. It will certainly keep you better nourished. The things we are likely to discuss at the supper table anchor our children more firmly in the world. Of course eating together teaches manners both trivial and momentous, putting you in touch with the deeper springs of human relations.[1]

I love what the first sentence of this impressive paragraph talks about: "eating the ordinary, average, everyday supper with your family." Nothing about gourmet here. The secret is the regularity and the togetherness. Actually getting to the table together is the real challenge.

I know regularity may not have been the norm for you, but it was a fine art practiced in my childhood home in Topeka. My father got home from work every evening at 5:30 p.m., in time to sip a cocktail and watch both the local and the national evening news. Dinner was served promptly afterward by my mother. The five of us sat down to meat with gravy or ketchup, potatoes, a vegetable, white bread with butter, and a glass of milk or iced tea. I don't remember even one exciting evening of this. But it still gets high marks for regularity.

Imagine the possibilities if variety, fun, *joie de vivre* were mixed in with that regularity on a regular basis. Imagine if the family experienced the consistency of the above scenario—and had a great time together besides! And let's say, to be more realistic for today, that we were to attempt to capture this four times a week. Or three times a week. Or even consistently two evenings a week. How are we going to get there?

If You Can Read, You Can Cook

What's your confidence level in cooking? If it's below a three on the one-to-five scale, maybe you're being too hard on yourself. Cooking is honestly just a matter of following the directions, then ad-libbing only if you feel like it. I distinctly remember that when I was an adult starting to cook, I had to look up how to hard-boil eggs. If I can write cookbooks today, you can cook.

If you don't know what to fix, find one or two ingredients in the pantry, then find a website that gives you a plethora of recipe options with them. Or browse through a cookbook. Honestly, a lot of cooking is just making up your mind to do it and doing the best you can with the ingredients and the energy you have on hand. Or have your husband or an older child do it, and

BECCA'S KITCHEN EQUIPMENT TIPS

You really just need two good knives, one large and one small, that you keep sharp and that cut well.

Your hands are great for juicing, straining, tossing, and mixing!

You don't need all those gadgets. You don't need a garlic press. Take the back of a knife and whack the garlic clove.

You don't have to use china just for its intended purpose. I use big white coffee mugs for soup and pasta bowls for hors d'oeuvres.

Purchase a few interesting serving pieces that you love, like one nice platter. You can slice your meat and put vegetables on one side and the meat on the other.

Purchase nice pots and pans you can put on your counter and serve from.

encourage them to have some fun with the process. There are several great cookbooks for kids, with pictures, that might be a good motivator for your child. Maybe Dad would also enjoy a cookbook that played to his specialty, whatever that may be.

The Magic *P* Word

Here is a list of usual mealtime roadblocks: *I don't have time to go to the store. I don't have time to prepare the meal. I'm too tired. I have places I need to go. Various family members will be missing, so the effort doesn't seem worthwhile.*

This whole bundle can be methodically attacked with an application of the magic *p* word—*planning*! So potent is the power of the magic *p* word that even in small applications it is effective. Meal planning is basically taking a step back to assess the upcoming situation so you can be prepared for it. Planning allows you to step back from the urgency of the next meal and put it in the perspective of the rest of the day or week. Even simply deciding that each day you'll determine before 9:00 a.m. what the family will eat for dinner that night gives you time to thaw something, sandwich a grocery trip into the day, figure out the most likely time to accomplish a meal together, and alert family members of that time.

A larger, even more effective stride is weekly meal planning. If you plot a week's meals on the calendar, noting free spaces when you'll all be going out, detours when you'll need a meal for the kids and a babysitter, or pile-ons when you'll add company, you'll be able to avert nothing-on-hand-to-eat crises and cut down on trips to the supermarket.

Stephanie R. enjoys the process of making a meal plan for the week. "I love to collect recipes and cookbooks and all that," she says. "It's fun to try new things. . . . I love knowing I have everything I need in my refrigerator. The family loves it. When I pick up the boys from school, they ask, 'What's for dinner, Mom?'" Her family uses a dinner bell to call everyone to the table—Caroline, age five, loves to ring it. And they come right away! In the past Stephanie would call, "Dinner . . . come on . . . come on!" But the dinner bell works.

It's so easy to fall back into the taco, pizza, spaghetti ruts. Not that they aren't okay. But if this rut is discouraging you or your family, you could create a list of family other-than-these favorites and tape it inside a cupboard door. Or tape up a list of some favorite seasonal recipes that take advantage of fruits and vegetables at their peak deliciousness. It's June as I write this, and we've been enjoying a blueberry spinach salad—how healthy is that!—a very simple fresh blueberry pie, and fresh corn on the cob on the grill. My family doesn't mind if we repeat these dishes every couple of weeks, because as the season for these passes, we'll be on to twice-baked sweet potatoes and sautéed apples in the fall.

And if you are especially organized (or really want to be), if you want very much to facilitate consistent family gatherings around the table, and if you also really want to save money on food, you might try preparing more than one meal at a time. You can try methods found online, cooking in bulk in food preparation businesses, or using the method found in *Once-a-Month Cooking*.[2]

Ultimate Planning

Once-a-Month Cooking is a book that gives you five menu options for preparing two weeks' or one month's dinner entrées in a day and freezing them. It saves your time, money, and energy and is the only book I know of that has been featured in both *Focus on the Family* magazine and the *National Enquirer*.

My friend Mimi Wilson devised "the method" when we had three young children each and were writing magazine articles together. She called me one day to tell me she'd figured out how to put together thirty entrées in one day and freeze them. Mimi loves to have company, and having the entrée already prepared was a huge help to her.

She asked me if I would call the *Denver Post* to see if they wanted us to write an article about it. I thought she was out of her mind and asked her to call them herself. They sent a reporter and photographer to her home within the week to do a food feature and, as they say, the rest, twenty-five years and several versions later, is history. And that history includes lots of adventures, like the time Mimi's physician husband Cal trekked into the jungle in Peru to treat a people group dying of pneumonia. His team was running out of food by the third day, but never fear, Mimi had an entrée-filled freezer even in Peru. She wrapped newspaper around the Tupperware containers and took them to the missionary pilot at the nearest airstrip so that he could fly over and drop them to the hungry medical team in the jungle. We call this episode "Bombs Away."

Mimi is the ultimate meal planner, and she has been a mentor to me in many other ways as well. Her kids are older than mine—her youngest the age of my oldest—and she was a mom I watched because I admired the way she spoke to her children, her tone of voice. I admired the way she disciplined them—and it generally seemed to work. I admired her solidarity in her marriage. She was always "for" Cal. If you can identify such a mentor in your life, they may help you with many aspects of your life—from mealtimes to marriage.

Finding the Table

Do you remember the poignant scene in the movie *The Passion of the Christ*, the lightest scene in the film, where the young carpenter Jesus fashioned something new—a high table you sat at and rested your elbows upon—and his mother shook her head in wonder?

I don't know just how far back the invention of the table reaches, but it seems to me to serve three purposes well: One, it holds the dishes, glasses, and utensils so you don't have to eat nervously, afraid you'll spill. Two, it arranges the eaters in a configuration where they can see one another. As Mimi says, "There's something about having everyone around the same table. You can keep your eye on them, to see they're all right." And three, the table provides a palette for color and pattern and three-dimensional beauty, especially in the little free space in the center.

Do you have a table for eating around? If you do, can you find the surface to set it, or is it routinely covered with bills and the things your home has sucked in that day that you don't have the energy to put away? It's a life principle that the best things are things we have to keep fighting for. The kind of healthy, regular family table time that our researchers described is one of those best things. To help keep the table clear, identify a different piling zone or set the table well before the meal so that family members see that there's a plan for that space (one that they will eagerly anticipate) and drop the backpacks elsewhere.

Our breakfast room table was purchased for us by my parents the first time they came to visit us after we were married—and saw that we ate on a card table. It is an oval wooden table treated with Formica on top, and I remember it was a big decision whether they'd purchase four chairs or six. Fortunately, they sprang for six.

It's still in good shape, although the finish on the chair seats is scraped from the wear and tear of booster seats. The table surface is marred by a spot of model paint, plus a dig from a pumpkin-carving knife. And, best of all, around it are the ghosts of lots of good mealtime memories.

Coming to the Table

Chrissy struggled with a disintegrating marriage, but somehow she knew, even without seeing the research, that eating at the table was important for her family. "I prefer everybody to sit at the table. Their dad would go to the couch and turn on the TV. Then I'd be the bad guy. But I'd try to sit and at least have conversations with the kids. We now [after the couple's separation] sit at the table, even with drive-through food. Sometimes I'll join the kids at a three-foot craft table, because it's more fun." A happier ending would have been that table times together became a healing time for this family. But the fact is that within the present state of affairs, Chrissy is giving a fixed point of stability to her children.

When Alex was traveling several weeknights a month and the boys were little, dinnertime was tedious, more ordeal than fun. Fortunately, I had a friend nearby, also with three little boys, whose husband traveled too. Once a week one of us called the other. We'd pool our leftovers, wear our comfy sweats, and eat together. After dinner the boys played, we talked over tea, and the evening slipped quickly and pleasantly to bedtime. Do what you need to do to make mealtimes work.

Watching TV during dinner can be a problem because you get to know the TV family better than your own. You're facing toward the TV and don't talk to each other. In fact, the family member who talks during the show is practically booed. If your family enjoys watching TV while you eat, you may want to approach withdrawal gradually. Two nights a week, turn it off. Then three nights. Eventually you'll have so much fun, you won't miss it.

It's different if you are eating alone. Then the TV can be good company—well, company anyway. But so can reading a book. Or changing your location so you're sitting on the porch watching birds at a feeder. Even a very simple meal is more special if we aren't haphazard about where we eat it and are connecting while we do.

Making Meals Meaningful

When your family is gathered around the table, how can you make this together time meaningful?

For some families the first thing that happens is the saying of a mealtime grace, a prayer of thanksgiving to God for the food. If you are people of faith, I would so encourage you to develop this as a habit so ingrained that it is automatically what you do first. Saying grace starts everyone off eating at the same time, which is good manners, and also helps you rope in stragglers to the table, because you're all waiting on them. Saying grace also prompts an attitude of gratefulness. We're thankful for food each meal, each day. We're thankful that someone took the time to prepare it or at least to bring it to us. We sense a "bigger than we are" element. God cares for our needs; we are thankful.

Saying grace can be, frankly, both interesting and fun. It's interesting because, especially if it is your family's custom to take turns praying "free form" prayers, sometimes prayers will be particularly touching and poignant or revealing as to the person's mood or state of heart. Prayer at the table together can reveal conflict or discontent. It can also help calm the ripples, especially if everyone has to hold hands and pray.

Saying grace can be fun because you never know what might come out. Even if your family prays a standard prayer of thanksgiving, it need not be a static ritual at all! Kim's family begins their meals with this prayer: *"Bless, O Lord, this food to our use and us to thy loving service. Give us grateful hearts and make us ever mindful of the needs of others."* But the manner in which they say it can vary. Sometimes they chant it. Sometimes they cheer it. Sometimes they get a little silly, but not irreverently so—just enjoying the experience. I would encourage you to pursue the practice of regularly saying grace before meals.

Mimi, my mentor, taught me a trick for making mealtimes memorable that is wondrously simple and nearly always sparks good results. She calls it putting a question on the table. Just think of a question for which there is no right or wrong answer and for which everyone old enough to talk will have an answer. Something like, "What do you like best about Grandma's house?" or "What do you think about when you're alone in the dark?" Don't you wonder what your family members would answer? Invariably we learn things about each other when we put a question on the table. The ground rule is that there are no stupid answers. Siblings can't shoot down the input of the others.

Show-and-tell works well at the table too—a child's drawing, a poem, a quote to discuss, an atlas and discussion of a part of the world in the news, an award won, a card received from a friend far away. This connecting is every bit as important in sad times as in times when someone is celebrating.

Brandy says of her home, "My big thing is to turn the TV off, and I like to have some music on just so we can sit and talk about the day. It's always what's going on with the girls at school and if they've had any problems or what good's happened today. My six-year-old likes to ask, 'What did you do nice for somebody today?' It's her favorite question. She asks everybody at the dinner table."

I've found that what regularly makes time around the table fun is attitude. It's constantly fighting the voice inside that says, *I finally have them all together, so I'll be sure they know how upset I am that the house is so messy.* Or, *Daddy needs to know how many times Jason talked back to me today*. It's a positive attitude that jumps the tracks of deep-conversation ruts: what happened at work today, how many times your mother-in-law called, which child has been misbehaving.

A good attitude wants to take advantage of the fact that for this brief respite, we are all together and can share who we are, how we're doing, and what's going on in our separate worlds. We're at home together around the table, and that's a good thing.

The attitude can be carried over to a centerpiece and table decoration. Fresh flowers make a "wow" centerpiece, but an interesting one might be an unusual piece of pottery, or a Barbie in an eclectic outfit, or a collection of autumn leaves or seashells. And add candles—not just for company. Kids love candlelight too. Making the table special adds to the appeal of eating together.

If you doubt for a minute the significance of the contribution to a home made by preparing regular meals, here is some encouragement from author Edith Schaeffer:

> To blend together a family group, to help human beings of five, ten, fifteen and sixty years of age to live in communication with each other and to develop into a "family unit" with constantly growing appreciation of each other and of the "unit" by really working at it, in many different areas, but among others in the area of food preparation, is to do that which surely can compare with blending oils in a painting or writing notes for a symphony. The cook in the home has opportunity to be doing something very real in the area of making good human relationships.[3]

Just think how important you are—in the difficult, creative, important work of claiming some meaningful family mealtimes.

Table Manners

I met a corporate trainer who said that the topic she is asked to present most often is basic table etiquette for the young executive, including how to carry on dinner conversation. I can't say that I learned the fine art of dining during those oh-so-regular dinners in Topeka. And as I grew up, frankly, I wished that I had. Like when I was sixteen and had a date with a boy from Florida who took me to a nice restaurant and ordered lobster. I'm quite sure I had never seen a lobster, much less eaten one. I gamely tried to cut some bites, shredding, unbeknownst to me, against the grain. Finally my golden boy leaned across the table and inquired, "May I help you cut that before you make me sick?"

Then there was the time in Paris when I was twenty-one. My three friends and I had just sat down to an elegant dinner when the waiter appeared and—ooh la la!—flicked open the linen napkin of the friend on my left and spread it ceremoniously across her lap. Well, I had never seen such a gesture, and it gave me the giggles. Uncontrollable giggles. As the poor fellow worked his way around, finally to me, I couldn't stop laughing. It destroyed any semblance of the sophistication I was attempting.

You might not know how to cut lobster or which fork to use when there are three in your place setting to choose from. And maybe you'll never need to know. But maybe you will, and maybe your children will. It's fun to research and practice table manners and to learn from people you eat with who are a bit more adept at such things than you are. Home is the place to learn manners for when we're not at home and need to know them. When we're confident about how to behave at a table, we can be at ease and attentive to the people we're with.

Strength from the Table

Holly told me that when her husband Wayne died suddenly in an accident, for several months the hardest thing for her and her three young children to do was to eat together at the table. They avoided it because Wayne's absence was so tangible there. But Holly gradually came to the conclusion that it was best that they did eat at the table, because they needed to grow to a healthy acceptance of their new family identity. This collection of people around the table was now their family. They began to build that understanding and also happier regular times together.

Families gain strength and learn gratitude from their times together at a family table. Vicki comments on this: "One of the most important factors is just loving the people who live there. We have a long list of things we want to do to the house, and I get frustrated because we just have to wait. But you know what? My kids are happy. My husband is happy. Everything functions. It's okay. It's not the end of the world. My laminate counters just don't matter. The kids couldn't care less. My daughter Bethany, each night when she says grace, prays, 'Thank you for this nice, cozy house.' She always says that." One winter night when Alex was unemployed, I was struck by the contrast of the cold, pitch dark outside the breakfast room window and the warm glow of the lamp over our table. We enjoyed the richness of each other and a warm meal, and the strength of our blessings overwhelmed the fearful unknowns.

The strength that comes from the regular family table, as our researchers said, radiates outward in many directions. When Mimi and Cal lived in Quito, Ecuador, Cal was initiating family practice as a specialty at the hospital. Cal and Mimi frequently entertained wealthy, professional Ecuadorians in their home, with house staff suitable to what this entailed. But Mimi's heart was equally with the people around their table and the people in the streets. Their home, like the others around it, was encircled by high walls topped with broken glass or barbed wire. But every evening Mimi made sure that a plate of leftovers—not a paper plate but a china plate with a napkin and utensils—was placed on a ledge just outside their back gate. The meal was always consumed. The plate, napkin, and utensils were always left in place.

In the Scriptures Jesus said that he values acts of kindness shown to people who are poor or devalued just as if the kindness had been done to him (see Matt. 25:40). In that respect, which facet of Mimi's entertaining was of the greatest value? It reminds me of giving a warm chocolate chip cookie to a boy named Joseph who showed up at the front door. Family meals provide nourishment from which we grow and provide simple opportunities for us to give.

When the day came for Alex and me to deliver Tim to begin college in Wyoming, I expected to be very emotional. Our oldest was leaving the nest. But the day was full of adventure and new horizons and went happily, even as Alex and I drove home.

Then that evening, as I set the table for dinner, it occurred to me that I could remove Tim's chair. That fifth chair had always made it tight on one side. As I gripped the back of it and tried to figure out the best place to put it . . . that's when the emotion got to me. I was physically removing someone from the circle that was us, our family, night after night. And although he would be back, I knew this was the beginning of significant change.

Keep in mind that even if we are committed to having a meal on an actual table with all the players present on a regular basis, it won't always be golden. There will be nights when people are just cross with each other and there doesn't seem to be any way around it. There will be nights when the meal really doesn't taste good. At all. And there will be nights like the one when Alex was out of town and the boys and I were eating a chicken casserole that included sliced water chestnuts. One of the boys observed that they resembled miniature Frisbees that needed to be thrown to one another. And the louder I tried to stop it, the more gleefully they laughed. There will be lots of nights like these.

But over the long haul—and we create homes for the long haul—there will be enough golden times that your family will eagerly gather from around the globe for a few more of them. Investment in regular family mealtimes at home is worth the price. Just do it.

Home Tour: Monday Night Is Family Night

Phil and Cathy's family includes seven children (five of them still living at home) and five grandchildren. When they sit at a table together, they number sixteen. It seats ten, but they make it fit thirteen and add two high chairs and a walker. And Cathy sees that all sixteen do sit at her table together—every Monday night.

Cathy cooks up the family's favorite foods, and they can't resist coming. Her motive at first was to see that the kids had a quality, regular time to connect with their dad, who is a pastor and so often busy with other families and their problems. They keep this time fun, and the food is plentiful and delicious. Of a Latino heritage, the family especially loves Cathy's Mexican food: burritos, enchiladas, and soft tacos. But she changes it up with lasagna or homemade pizza, or sometimes egg rolls and fried rice.

Doesn't she get tired of preparing that huge meal herself, every week? "No," Cathy says, smiling. "I love to cook. To me it's so well worth it to have everybody get together." Sometimes the guys of the family have a harder time making it priority—until Cathy announces what she'll be serving for dinner. Somehow cooking their favorites always gets them there.

Play and Rest

Homes take naps while their people and their pets are away. They rest. They stay clean if they were left clean, stay messy if left messy. When you open the door again, the condensed smell of your home meets you. Your home's smell has been distilling and magnifying in thick, still air. Homes have their opportunities to rest.

The Home at Play

But do homes play? Magazine homes don't play. They are stiff and too ready for our viewing. Crews have worked hours to be sure each accessory is au courant and exactly in place. But do real-life homes play?

They certainly *contain* our family play, and perhaps they absorb it and bounce it back and forth from wall to wall. And a home is playful when it contains some whimsy, some personality, some "I'm ready for play—just try me." A home that is set up for play, that makes us inclined to play, plays too.

Julie's family has a playful kitchen. Hanging by the kitchen table, where they can see it often and enjoy it, is what Julie calls the "evolving painting." It's a huge canvas that they periodically take out to the garage and paint all over again. The whole family. With no particular plan in mind. "It's probably got about four hundred layers of paint on it now, but we all work together on it," Julie says. "My husband doesn't much, but the kids and I do a lot. It's always changing. It changes color, whatever we're in the mood for. And we leave it up anywhere from a week to six months, until we get tired of it, and then we change it again." It's cheap, it's fun, and visitors don't know what to expect it to be next when they come to Julie's home.

In Rita's home a floor-to-ceiling bulletin board serves as a changing autobiography of the house. It is overflowing with family art, photos (and don't we often take photos because we're playing?), original poems, jokes, and top-ten lists.

A home pictured in a magazine includes a craft storage area straddling a mud room sink. Under the countertops are drawers and large, open cubbyholes for storing supplies. A shelf above the sink flaunts finished children's art. What fun! It makes me want to grab a smock, paint, and brushes. This room wants to include me in its play.

In Stephanie R.'s home, the piano that she grew up playing is in a small room close to the kitchen. "Sometimes we have a guest over who knows how to play. It's neat when someone can just sit down and play," she says. The piano is located where the guest is likely to see it, sit down, and tickle the ivories.

Nearby, their kitchen holds three stools for the kids, and the built-in baskets designed for potatoes hold paper and markers instead. "That's part of a home—seeing that your kids have what they need to be creative," says Stephanie. Six-year-old Caroline dances in the kitchen and watches her reflection in the glass door while her brothers color at the counter. A kitchen bench holds science project supplies and puzzles.

I can still hear in my mind the sound of our son Dan rooting through a drawer of Legos to find just the right one. We kept an old dresser in the basement family room. Once a Lego set had been mixed up with its cousin Lego sets, they were housed together in the dresser drawers. The kids could remove the drawers and set them on the floor for closer scrutiny. Cleanup was a snap: back into the drawers they went.

At Christmastime we like to keep up a jigsaw puzzle. Inevitably there are guests or family members who like to sit alone at the card table or work quietly in twos to see the scene take shape. Puzzles for young children could be kept nearby.

The home that is set up for play, that begs you to come play, will be played in.

The Ways We Play

Some of you, like me, need a refresher on what it means—literally—to play. So from *The New Oxford American Dictionary* we discover:

> play: engage in activity for enjoyment and recreation rather than a serious or practical purpose

As we see quite plainly, play does not encompass multitasking. It only allows me to be mildly competitive. It's not meant to accomplish anything. It's supposed to be fun. There can be no losers in play; there are no big behind-the-scenes objectives for someone to thwart. The old adage claims that the family that plays together, stays together. That makes sense to me. When they play at home, family members will be more likely to hang out together and to come home more often—because it's fun!

Do you play at home? How do you play? Steph, a single mom, has found a way to play with five-year-old Sean after work that is fun for them both: "I get out of my work clothes right away. I get into a comfy T-shirt and sweatpants. Put my hair up in pony tails. When it's nice, Sean and I go for a walk. He goes for

THE LOGAN FAMILY THEATER

The four children in the Logan family enjoy staging plays together and with neighborhood friends. Steve, the dad, constructed a theater in the basement using a double-door walk-in cedar closet as the starting point.

When the closet doors are open, curtains on a rod cover the opening. The closet becomes a backstage area to hold costumes and props and for an exit off the stage.

Steve constructed a wooden frame that extends five feet into the room on either side of the closet doors and spans ten feet across the front. Curtain rods around this area hold curtains that can be opened by pulling a string. Rows of folding chairs face the stage.

The two older girls write the scripts. They take existing shows like *The Wizard of Oz* or *Peter Pan*, add songs from unrelated shows or artists that "fit" somehow, and work it all together into scripts. All interested children audition for parts. Costume construction is part of the fun, and mom Jennifer helps when necessary.

Finally comes the satisfaction of performing for an enthusiastic audience of family and friends of all ages!

a bike ride while I walk. [It's the] first thing we do before the sun goes down."

To Mary, quilting is play: "I quilt during the day because I need the light. You make too many mistakes when it's dark. So it comes in competition with doing errands, doing the boring things like going to the grocery store. And it wins out a lot. The most creative part is planning it. But I also enjoy the technical part of getting it just right. Even the dogs have a quilt. So many techniques. So many new things coming up!" A hobby like quilting, one that you love to do so much that it crowds out the daily boring stuff, is play.

Brandy's family likes to play board games together. "Last Christmas," says Brandy, "I found a couple of really neat games. . . . One is called Walk the Dog, and it's all these miniature plastic dogs that you line up in this big trail on the floor, and you pull cards and build your own little trail of dogs. The kids love Chutes and Ladders, charades—we have a Disney charades game that they really like. My older daughter really likes Monopoly. The six-year-old's getting there, but she still doesn't get the money yet." If you have a wide age range at home, playing board games in teams is a good way to keep the odds even.

Stephanie R. and Charlie live in a remote, wooded area, and Charlie has set up targets back in the woods. He likes to take the kids or guests out on their back deck to practice archery with bows and arrows.

T. J. and Meredith work hard at helping their children find play away from the TV. They have a great relationship with their neighbors, who also have young children, so between the two families they have set up different types of play equipment: T. J. and Meredith have a trampoline and sandbox, and the neighbors have a play set; they installed a gate between the two yards for easy access between them. "The kids still have to ask to come over, but we encourage them to play with each other," T. J. says.

The backyard set up for home play helps them in their quest to keep from overscheduling Jackson, age three, and Grace, age five. They're not in soccer or T-ball, although Grace has taken ballet. They swim lots as a family. "It's our philosophy to not be too busy while they're young. We've decided to not do some of that stuff—just let them play. We don't have a little Tiger Woods here. And we do like keeping it simple. Just hanging out in the back yard. It's fun. I don't like having things scheduled," T. J. says.

T. J. and Meredith find that home is a good place to play. Instead of an $80 night with dinner, a movie, and a babysitter, they often opt to get the kids to bed by 8:00 or 8:30 p.m., stay up late gabbing, and sometimes watch a movie. It's their time.

Rest

Until I checked the definitions of play and rest, they mushed together in my mind. The main difference, I've found, is that play has an element of activity, and rest ceases to be active. Again, according to the dictionary:

> rest: cease work or movement in order to relax, refresh oneself, or recover strength

Still, many things could go both ways. What is knitting—play or rest? Actually, when play is restful and rest is playful, isn't that just the best?

Let's look at the home that is not napping, with its people and pets away, but rather that helps us nap, helps us rest.

The Home at Rest

A home is a bundle of sensory experience in which we wrap ourselves. The sounds, smells, sights, touches, and tastes of home can be conducive to rest—or not!

Take the sounds of home, for example. One of the most restful sounds of our home comes from Alex's water feature trickling over stones to the basin pool below. The water trickles over only three levels of rock, and the pool is small. The sound is quiet, unpretentious, just right.

Restful sound is usually low volume and sends the heart rate down, not up. In Cathy A.'s home all of the kids play the piano, several of them by ear. That means, with seven kids, often someone is playing the piano. One son is particularly gifted. Some nights Phil, a busy urban pastor, will come home, sit in the living room, and ask his son to please play for him. It's so soothing and gives him lots of peace. Music can evoke all kinds of moods, including restfulness at the heart of the home.

The aroma of honeysuckle blooms helps make Carla's front porch her family's favorite place for rest. They live in a 1920s bungalow in the city with a porch across the front and a city sidewalk a few feet away. "I plant my garden so there are things to enjoy from the porch," says Carla. On summer evenings a family member or two often sit reading in the cool air. Their neighbors across the street have a porch too, and they say hi or walk over to talk. In June the honeysuckle vine blooms on the front fence. Its sweetness can be smelled from the porch and from the sidewalk. "People walk by the honeysuckle a little slower," says Carla. "It's like an oasis."

One reason Carla likes the porch, versus sitting inside the house, is that it is removed from the "to dos" of home. "I can't hear the phone," she says. "I don't see the mail and bills; I don't see the stack of newspapers or various piles of stuff from the family that get spread around the living, dining, kitchen areas of the home. Of course, there are weeds in the garden, but somehow they don't bother me as much as all the 'to dos' inside the house."

I suspect that our universal love of snuggling under a blanket or throw for a nap or a movie or a cozy storytime echoes back to being swaddled as babies and dragging around "blankies" as toddlers. In one of his memorabilia boxes, our son Tim still has a small, ragged remnant of the yellow crocheted blanket that he loved to curl his fingers into when he sucked his thumb. Whether or not you had a blankie, you probably can't resist one on a sofa or cushy chair when you're leaning toward a nap—and it takes you over the edge into slumber.

Do you have a special resting place in your home? A reclining chair, or a hammock, or a window seat with pillows, or a rocking chair, or a swing on the porch? If not, you need to find one, stake your claim, and let it call you away to rest.

When we're resting, the tastes we reach for are usually sweet or salty, easy to prepare or grab, and not necessarily the best for us! But snacking on something yummy is an important part of rest. April's family rests in front of football or basketball games or NASCAR races with sodas and nachos or chips or popcorn. It's just part of the total package.

The Ways We Rest

One morning I woke up with no set alarm and no immediate agenda (other than coffee) and watched the changing pattern of the sunlight on the blinds and the fluttering leaves outside the window. The purity of it—the interchange of sunlight and shadow, the trembling flashes of green—left me perfectly content to neither rise nor sleep but simply to be.

Resting seems to me to be some of the hardest work I do, because I've so trained myself that at all times I must be "getting something done." I find myself being a counterfeit rester. For example, I've taken up knitting again. I've done this because I love the fun things I can make, the feel of the yarn in my fingers, the colors and pattern as the item takes shape, and just the satisfaction of creating. But I also face the subtle pressure to *complete one more row. Get this section done by Friday. Watch TV or talk to someone while I knit*. Ugh! So for me, a morning moment in bed watching the patterns of sunlight and shade is beautiful.

Tim coined an expression that is an apropos description of learning to rest: "trading paces." That's what we do when we rest. We trade an active, intentional pace for a passive, reflective one. In order to choose how we will rest, we must know ourselves well: what refuels us, refreshes us, makes us feel creative again. And keepers of homes need to know what refuels and refreshes our spouses and our children so we can help them get that rest. It includes being wary of the impediments that keep them, and us, from getting that rest. Alex needs to nap and ride his bike on Sunday afternoons without the impediment of honey-do chores. When the boys were little, I felt like whenever they really did rest, I had to yank them from the revelry to go on an errand or to an appointment. Truly I sometimes welcomed days when they were sick—if they weren't very sick—as a perfect excuse to be attentive to them and for all of us to slow down and just rest.

How do other families rest in their homes? Mimi, who has lived on four continents, embraces the wisdom of the British, who drink tea at 4:00 p.m., and of Latinos, who drink coffee. She has a break and "a little something," preferably with a friend, at that time of the day.

When we say that pets are good companions, a given is that their presence helps us rest. Annoying pets are overly demanding and don't help us rest.

A favorite family photo shows Drew at about eighteen months old, sitting on the sofa in footie pajamas with both big toes poking through (reminding me that he, as the third son, got double hand-me-downs). He is concentrating on the camera as he holds up Frisky the kitten by the neck in his two hands. In fact, this photo fits a theme running through the scrapbook: Frisky the kitten being run around the yard in Tippy the German shepherd's mouth. Frisky the cat curled around Timmy and his blanket, sleeping on the floor. Frisky and Tippy asleep on the floor together. Frisky perched (like she always did—looking like she was laying an egg) on the sofa back behind Uncle Don, who hates cats. Frisky was a terrific, affectionate cat. We've often thought it was because the boys were little when she was a kitten, and they held or handled her almost continually. We got a lot of play value out of Frisky, and she also helped us rest, because she loved to curl up next to or on top of anyone who was napping.

When Jane's family rests, they take the back cushions off their big sofa so they can all three lie down on it and watch a movie or read. They also go on leisurely walks. Or they just lie around and look at magazines or play with the dog.

Jane was put on bed rest for a surprise pregnancy in her forties. "Normally I would press on," said Jane. "I'm not good at knowing when to stop. But it taught me a valuable lesson. If I'm not 90 percent, then it overflows into our family. If I don't take care of myself, I'm not equipped to take care of anyone else. Now when I pass a limit, I know it's best for everyone that I take that hour."

As for bedtime, the process that lulls toward rest and sleep, Jane says, "We try to keep bedtime fairly consistent for all of us. The bedtime routines are significant: Around 8:00 p.m. is Sarah's bath time, and we totally start winding down. I read to Sarah, and we pray. Sometimes I'll lie down with her for a while. We already discussed highs and lows of the day at dinnertime. Bedtime consists of thanking God for the day. That's how we close our day together."

Brandy's family has a dedicated family night at least once or twice a month on Friday nights. "We watch movies," Brandy said. "Sometimes we have 'sleepovers,' we call them, in the family room where we all sleep on the floor and stay up and watch Nick@Nite or whatever."

T. J. and Meredith's young children sometimes watch the Noggins series on TV as time for rest. But the parents are cautious about other shows, even cartoons. "We don't like shows where they use bratty voices," said T. J. "Kids don't understand," explained Meredith. "They don't watch an entire thirty-minute program and see the moral. They're mimicking the voices and laughing if it's funny. They get up and leave before the end of it."

A group backrub can mellow any group to near wilting. Everyone sits on the floor in "choo-choo train" fashion, and each person rubs the back of the one in front of them. Then they turn around and rub backs the other way.

Finally, reading is rest. "Charlie and I love to read, lying in bed side by side, each having our own book," says Stephanie R. In the Moon family, dad Bill loves to read aloud to the family. When they travel, they like to listen to an audio book. They turn it off periodically to discuss a word the kids don't understand (Brandon is twelve and Kayley is eight) or to ask, "What do you think is going to happen?" or "Why do you think he was so upset?"

One time they finished a road trip but weren't yet at the end of their book, *Hatchet*. So they went into the house, lay down in the living room, and listened to the rest. They had to hear how it turned out! Book-resting together creates wonderful memories for a family.

Day of Rest

In my thinking, the commandments of God are markers pointing out for us the way life is hardwired: how to behave in order to live a life that is full and all that it was meant to be. So I take it seriously that God says we must rest. One day out of seven, we need to put down all the equipment and give it a rest. Life will go better.

But how does a family live out Sabbath, a day of rest, at home? Kurt and Lori see Sabbath as a fast from productivity. They don't turn on the computer. They don't answer the phone. After church Lori sometimes fixes a simple meal. In the summer they pack a picnic and go to the beach. Or they play a game with the kids. On cold winter days they might go sledding with friends and have hot chocolate together.

Kevin and Sarah, living in Peru, use a Sabbath for marriage maintenance. "As missionaries," says Kevin, "life is very invasive on personal space, personal time, family time." Sabbath felt like active defense of their marriage. They've stopped having people over on a Sabbath. "We thought that was part of it, but we've stopped. We sleep as late as we can. We try to have a date." Sarah adds, "One week Kevin will decide about our date, and the next week I will. That frees the other from the decision."

In Keri's home, she aims to keep the day simple. They go to church, and then she's available to the kids. Her husband Scott is a realtor and often isn't at home on Sunday afternoons.

One time Keri's son asked, "Mom, what do we have today?" (as in have to do today). Keri replied, "Aaron, it's Sunday. What do you think we have today?" Aaron thought a bit and said, "Peace." And Keri said, "You're right; that's what we have today. Peace." Her daughter has friends who like to come to their house on Sundays because it's peaceful. These are kids who are used to doing lots of things on the Sabbath.

"When I talk to moms of older kids who do Sabbath well, they try to be available in the home, but they don't make their kids stay home," says Keri. The kids come and go, but they know that if they need to talk to Keri, she's not going to be running around. "I'm not going to have the computer on," she says. "I'm not going to be doing laundry. I'm reading the Sunday *Tribune* or working in my garden, but I'm home and available to them, and if they want to talk to me they know it's not like, 'No, sorry, I'm on deadline.' I work from home. Sometimes I'm on deadline and I've got to work. Sunday's a day that doesn't happen. And so I'm just available. They don't have to stay [home], but usually they do. We have the board games right under the TV on a shelf. On Sundays if they want to play board games with me, I always say yes. I never say I'm too busy."

I admire these Sabbath-keeping stories. I respect the struggle it is to declare a Sabbath and to make it happen. In our home we have been moving that way so that Sunday morning includes worship and Sunday afternoons are open-ended and pleasantly spent in naps or reading the newspaper on the patio. For Alex it's riding his bike or watching sports on TV. I do know that first steps, even baby first steps, are important in launching into a new life pattern. A literal Sabbath-keeping is not the point; the point is developing a life pattern that makes space for regular periods of rejuvenating rest. It's the intentional pattern over a stretch of years that imprints a clear difference in the quality of life in a heart-healthy home.

Play and rest are fundamental to the health of home. Without both we grow stagnant and stodgy—and we grow apart. They keep life fresh in our homes.

Home Tour: Reading with the Moons

On a summer evening the Moon family ate a late dinner on their patio. As darkness fell and bedtime approached, the kids asked if they could put the patio chairs back in the reclining position, bring out pillows and blankets, and read aloud under the stars. Their family reads a lot together.

The mom, Kim, said later that fortunately she was able to go with this, to live in the present. So there they were: Bill, the dad, reading *The Lord of the Rings* by flashlight, with Kim in the patio chair next to him knitting. Brandon and Kayley looked at the stars and listened. The dog lay next to them in the yard. And neighbors walked by quietly, listening too.

As Kim said, "It was just so nice to be together. We weren't really expecting anything to happen; it wasn't planned. At Christmas we have elaborate expectations. Then when something goes wrong, it's upsetting because it's a lot of work. But this was allowing myself to be in the moment, to put those 'should' voices away."

Home Keeping

A friend brought me a little vase of flowers yesterday. Fresh flowers are a treat, and I walked from room to room with the vase, deciding where they would be enjoyed the most. I settled on an oval marble table in the living room between two comfy chairs, and I paused to open the blinds because the afternoon sunshine seemed to want to join in. I straightened magazines and plumped pillows, making the place look fitting for the little crown of flowers.

I've spent the summer months working and writing and away on weekends, and I miss my home. I miss the puttering in it that gives me a finger on the pulse of my family. Whether my home is peaceful or out of control usually reflects the state of the lives within it. And I even miss the cleaning that gets my home and me reacquainted.

I'm not too worried, though. There is a rhythm to a home and its care that adjusts to "seasons of imbalance." This major deadline will pass, and with the arrival of fall I hope to exchange the jonquils on the table for some bittersweet and sort out and mop thoroughly in the laundry room. There is a day-to-day pressure to keep a home clean and smoothly running that intensifies with the number of family members or the smallness of their age. But there is also a seasonal rhythm that allows us to correct the balance over time.

Your Cleanliness Style

We each fall at some point on a scale from messy to perfectionist, this being our cleanliness style. A good friend, who has seen all the places in my home I wouldn't want company to see, gave me as a gift a little plaque that reads, "Dull women have immaculate homes." I think she wanted to cheer me up. But of course there is really no correlation. My friend Chuck, who likes to hang his suits in his closet exactly an inch apart from each other as they are in the nice men's clothing stores, is not dull (I know, he's also not a woman, but bear with me), nor is his fetish for neatness more "right" than my habits are.

Often our cleaning habits and expectations are either trained by or in reaction to those of our parents. Chrissy says that in her parents' home, "all the counters, top of the refrigerator, everything is overflowing. I grew up like that, and I think that's what made me go in the other direction. When I got my own apartment, I didn't even want the toaster out."

Often we are not at the same place on the cleanliness scale as our spouse is. Talk about potential for continual conflict! Although neither partner is exactly "right," the fact is that we significantly affect each other's day-to-day lives by our expectations and standards of cleanliness. So later we'll look more closely at this delicate dance.

Strategies for Success

No matter your cleanliness style, I'm sure you would like to keep your home running smoothly and harmoniously. Here are several strategies that will help.

Routines

My dad, who enjoyed routines, rose each morning at the same early hour, and by the time I was up he was seated at the kitchen table in his "coffee pants" (a one-piece snap-up-the-front work outfit), double cowlicks frolicking in his dark hair as he drank coffee and read the morning paper. It was the routine that started his day off right.

Even for those of us who aren't given to routines, it pays to identify the biggest home maintenance challenges—those things that can sabotage home life and bring it to a standstill—and figure out some routines to help keep them under control. The three biggies, it seems to me, are food (purchasing, preparing, cleaning up); information (bills, papers to sign or file, phone calls, email); and clothing (purchasing, cleaning, maintaining). Routines are actually big time savers because you don't have to think so much. You don't have to make so many decisions. If you put in the thinking time initially to figure out a routine, then systems will generally run more smoothly.

Let's look briefly at each of these big three. Food is a topic we examined in chapter 4. The key is planning for as many days ahead as fits your family's needs and your style. For cleanup we might learn from brothers Jon and Nathan. They are very clear on what is expected of them. Jon says that he does the dishes on Friday and Sunday nights. Nathan does them on Wednesday and Saturday nights. I suspect that whichever one isn't doing the dishes sets the table. Their parents have found a system that is working great (and doesn't seem to be up for debate).

The constant flow of information to be processed, especially school papers and bills, is the second biggie. Kathy has mounted wall pockets from the office supply store on their mud room wall, one labeled for each of their four children, plus one labeled for her. Below the wall pockets are cubbies for the kids' backpacks. When they come home from school, the kids empty their backpacks of anything like field-trip permission forms that Kathy needs to sign. They put these items into Kathy's wall pocket. After she's signed them, she puts them in the appropriate child's wall pocket. The kids check their wall pockets as they grab their backpacks to go to school the next day. Slick, huh?

One simple idea for maintaining clothing is to hang your clothes according to color groupings. Once you set up the closet this way, it's easy to maintain it, and it saves lots of time pushing hangers back and forth looking for one particular green shirt. Actually, the closet looks much prettier too.

Pat keeps three big baskets in her laundry room: one for darks, one for lights, and one for heavies (like towels and jeans). Whenever she sees that one is full, she runs that load.

Kathy sorts and folds the clean laundry, then piles the clothes of each family member on the kitchen chairs where they usually sit. Before they sit down for dinner, each has to put his or her clothes away.

Food, information to process, and clothing are three areas that are worth your investment of time in developing routines to help you keep your home systems from bogging down.

Chunking

After routines, a second successful strategy touted by home-management authorities is to divide your tasks into chunks. That is, set a time limit for your chores, set an accomplishable goal, and when it's finished, it's finished. Chrissy, for example, does laundry on Mondays and Tuesdays. Whatever laundry is not washed, dried, and put away by the end of the day Tuesday will just have to wait until the next week (better wash underwear first!). She cleans bathrooms one day. She vacuums one day. Dusts one day. And she runs errands on a day when her children are at a play date. "I don't take my kids to the store," she says. "It adds up to fifty dollars more groceries in the cart." If Chrissy has sick children on both her vacuum and dusting days, she doesn't need to stack these chores onto her errands

TIPS FROM AN EXCELLENT CLEANING RESOURCE:
SPEED CLEANING BY JEFF CAMPBELL AND THE CLEAN TEAM[1]

Make every move count. That means work around the room once, carrying your equipment and supplies with you.

Use the right tools. Most of all, you need a cleaning apron to hang tools on and store cleaning supplies in as you move around the room.

Work from top to bottom.

If it isn't dirty, don't clean it. If all that's dirty about a surface is a few fingerprints, don't clean the whole area.

Keep your tools in impeccable shape.

Use both hands.

If there are more than one of you, work as a team.

day; she can tackle them even more thoroughly when those days roll around the next week. The object is to chip away at regular cleaning and maintenance tasks so that you feel like you're accomplishing something—even small-task somethings—instead of always feeling you're behind.

When you're thinking beyond house cleaning to sorting through and organizing, the chunking principle comes in handy. Tackle cleaning out one drawer or one closet at a time. You don't have to take on a whole room. As you clean out cupboards and closets, keep three bags at hand: one for items you want to put away in another room, one for items to give away, and one for trash.

Karen, who cleans houses for a living, talks about the difference between cleaning other people's houses and your own. "I've tried different formulas in my own home. In your own home you've got a lot of little things to deal with. It's not like going to another home. I can go in someone else's house and even if there are piles, I can work around them, and they don't slow me down. But in my own house I plan on cleaning the dining room or living room and the next thing I know I'm going through school papers." Before Karen cleans her own home, a bit of "pre-clean" picking up of papers to find the surfaces helps her work along smoothly on cleaning day.

Communicating

Brandy is a realtor, and she says a common observation about couples she helps look for a home is that they haven't really talked to each other before looking at homes with her. So when she asks them a question like, "What are your top five must-haves in a home?" they end up reacting to each other: "What? I didn't know you wanted that!" Cleaning and maintaining a home together is one of those many areas where just talking to each other helps. In sharing chores and responsibilities, for example, pick apart what tasks each of you doesn't mind or even likes to do.

Recently I've discovered that our son Tim really likes to go to the grocery store. I can hand him a list, and he'll return with a few selections that I wouldn't have tried but with basically the things on the list. Not only have I stayed out of the store, but I'm trying foods that I otherwise wouldn't have experienced. And the stretching experience is the trade-off for the convenience of his shopping—because in asking him to go, I've given up control. It's no fun for him if I expect him to do the task but give him no choices.

Maintaining a home involves all sorts of tasks that one spouse knows more about or does better than the other spouse, like getting on a ladder and cleaning out the gutters or changing the furnace filter or washing windows or hanging pictures. I have found that if Alex knows more about the task than I do and is willing to do it, I am wise to can the unsolicited advice and let him do it! Otherwise he probably won't do it, and then it defaults to me.

Whether it's children or a spouse we're asking to do chores, how we ask is supremely important. This is one of those times when too often you might hear your mother's tone of voice coming from your own mouth (with all due respect to your mother), or at least some unpleasant tone of voice. Here are strategies some moms have found to work with their kids.

Chrissy makes a game of cleanup time in the evening. Every night she sings the Barney cleanup song. Everybody is expected, during the song, to pick up their own stuff and put it away: shoes, jackets, cups, toys. She keeps a large basket in the family room in which they can put toys they've brought from their bedrooms. Once a month each of the kids gets a shopping bag to "shop" for their own toys from the basket and go put them away. Chrissy also keeps bins for certain types of toys like Legos and Barbies. She says, "I notice the kids will play with their things more [using the bins]. If their room is chaos, they won't go in their room. If it's clean and they know where things are, they'll grab it down."

For Alice's houseful of kids, "charts or schedules never worked," she says. So she used to require them to clean up their rooms before they participated in a special activity.

When it's Alex I'm asking for help, I've learned that he likes to have me prepare a (short) list of what I'd like him to do, preferably the day before or the morning of, so he can prioritize and plan the tasks into his day—or tell me if he won't have time or would rather not do them. We can talk about the tasks written down, and it makes the process more objective.

Rachel, who lives in a house with three roommates, uses humor to keep one roommate's stuff from invading the space of all the others. "I have one roommate who finds different things and purchases them a lot. Like luggage, or blankets, or air mattresses. Fortunately, she has the largest room, so a lot of it stays in her room, and there's a storage area in the basement. But we tease her a lot. We'll say, 'Okay, enough of the air mattresses. Okay, no more luggage.'" Rachel and her roommates are able to communicate their concern about the overflow without rankling the other roommate.

Purging

Some days I look around my home and wonder, *How does all this stuff get here?* On any one day we don't bring much into the house. Where does it come from? The more stuff we have, the more we have to take care of. And the harder it is to keep the house picked up.

Periodic exfoliation is necessary. It is typically initiated by the spouse most bothered by clutter. But it can be a real battle in families with sentimental packrats. Alex wants to keep, for example, the large shoebox of forty golf balls from the driving range where he worked when he was a teenager. I'm thinking four golf balls can elicit an equal degree of nostalgia, but the box in the garage makes the cut year after year.

When things have gotten out of hand and purging is really necessary (according to me), events like this have proven to work well: We'll have what I call a Great Garage Cleanout, with notice of a week or two ahead, or a Great Camping Equipment Cleanout. Twice a year, in the fall and the spring, we have the Great Clothes Closet Cleanout. You get the idea.

Our daughter-in-law came over as we were having one of the garage extravaganzas, with everything from the garage pulled out into the yard and driveway for purging and reorganizing, and she commented that it looked like our garage had vomited. And so it did.

These events are most productive if they are carefully orchestrated to come just before a neighborhood garage sale or on the weekend before a scheduled "used items" pickup. Dispersal must take place quickly, or the stuff is assimilated back into its old places. Other places that welcome your unwanted items are clothing consignment stores, your local library, and women's crisis shelters. Some churches have bins for dropping off unwanted cell phones, hearing aids, and eye glasses. Other people may value many of the things that you don't anymore.

Get Help When You Need It

At various times and for various reasons we all could use some help at home. Sometimes we're able to pay for help; sometimes we need to just ask it of family and friends. Jane, who was pregnant and weary in her midforties, has a new attitude about asking for help. She says that after the baby is born, she will get some help. She'll pay someone to clean, and she'll ask friends and family to come in sometimes and take the baby for a while so she can rest, and also so she can stay connected to her ten-year-old daughter, who had not expected to have a sibling. "We have church, Sunday school people who have expressed interest," she says. "I will call. I wouldn't have some years ago. But if someone called me and said they were at their wit's end and needed help, I would go in a heartbeat. I have to believe they would for me too."

Paying for help with cleaning and household tasks is a time and money balance. Do you have the time to complete what is necessary but not the money? Or do you have the money but not the time? Sometimes paying for a slightly older neighbor child to play with your children while you clean is just the help you need. They generally enjoy receiving any little bit you can pay them.

Keeping Up on Home Maintenance

Craig is a contractor who built his own home from scratch—a very handy guy. Craig believes in the adage that if something is worth doing, it's worth doing right. A repair done correctly will save time, money, and headaches in the years to come. Think of the story of the three little pigs. The first built his house of sticks, and the big bad wolf huffed and puffed and blew it down—and ate the pig (in the original version of the story). The second little pig built his house of twigs, with the same result. The third little pig built his house of bricks and sat in an armchair by the fire as the wolf blew his worst unproductively. It's also like the biblical story of the man who built his house on the sand versus the one who built on a rock (see Matt. 7:24–27). When the rain came and the wind rose, the house on the sand was washed away, but the house on the rock stood sound. When we choose our home's building materials well and then maintain it consistently, our little piggies are comfy and safe inside as the elements howl away.

When it comes to home maintenance, Craig says it's important to not put off repairs when you notice little things. Like with plumbing. It's usually hidden in a cabinet, and as long as the faucet works, you think everything's fine. But look underneath the sinks periodically, not just for puddles of water but for corrosion. If you see calcium buildup around the pipes, there's a leak. The water may be evaporating and not dripping yet.

Another example of an important thing to maintain is the furnace. Changing the filter frequently can in the long run save you the motor. Pressure builds up if the air doesn't flow; that makes the motor work harder and go out quicker. Craig recommends also learning to spot carbon buildup around the thermocouple.

Doing your own home repairs is much cheaper, but if you're not particularly handy or home repair savvy, just learn to be observant and ask questions, Craig says. If a repair person comes to your home, stick with him, ask lots of questions, and have him show you things. "You build this knowledge based upon observation and questions, not because somebody trained you to do it," he says.

Craig did this with his children when they were small and he was building their home. Even when they were two and three years old, Craig involved them in the process. "They absorb a lot, and then it's not a scary deal. When there's no conversation about it, they have no basis to start with, and it's a big mystery."

In the interior of your home, most of the wear and tear will be from appliances and mechanical things. The rest is aesthetics.

As far as exterior maintenance goes, Craig maintains that

painting is number one. Check your wood surfaces, he says. Check up close, not just from the street. Keep paint and caulk in good shape so water doesn't get underneath the paint.

Beyond paint, check for gaps in caulking. Caulk is supposed to bond with whatever surfaces you have. Nails can work their way out and loosen the trim and siding. Replace them with screws that will pull it back in. Craig says, "If you just hit the nail back in, you're putting it back into the hole it slid out of." Being proactive and doing it right can go a long way toward keeping your home in good repair.

The Happy Side of Housework

Housework has its happy sides. It's a pleasant thing to make your home environment look its best. It's satisfying to welcome friends into a freshly scrubbed kitchen or to watch children push toy cars around on a clean carpet. It feels good to walk into your home when it's clean and neat.

Some chores may be cathartic for you, like sweeping the porch on a warm spring day or shaking out a tablecloth under the stars as you catch your breath after having company.

Maintaining a home is a continuous task but not without its rewards. Do what you can, in the rhythm of your life's seasons, to make your home look good. With the help of family teamwork, your home will run smoothly and look its best.

Home Tour: Craig and Debbie Remodel

To start their home remodel, Craig and Debbie sat down and listed all the things they wanted to do, without considering the cost. Then from this list they prioritized. What changes were most important to them?

They created their budget, realizing that costs for remodeling projects often run over anticipated expenses by 20 percent. Often when you get into a project, one thing leads to another that you hadn't anticipated. Or it becomes more expensive than anticipated to "do it right."

With their budget, Craig and Debbie pared down the list. If they couldn't afford an item on the list, they went down to the next one.

As they dreamed, they didn't restrict themselves to the space they already had. Exterior walls are limiting, but interior walls can be changed.

Craig and Debbie's goal was to update their home. "At our age you feel like you can get into a grind," Craig says. "It brings a new energy to things [to remodel]. It invigorates your marriage. It invigorates you. There's a sense of newness that you feel by redecorating. It's restorative."

"It gives us a chance to dream together again. Yes, it can be stressful because of the decision-making process you have to go through. But because it gives you a chance to dream together again . . . it makes you look forward to the future instead of living for today. You see how it can be used in a different way. . . . I guess for us it's been the dream you kind of dream together again. When you get busy you don't do that anymore."

Geography of Home

Not everyone considers home the structure in which they currently live, or even vaguely "wherever the family is." For some people home is a fixed spot on the map that does not change with years and circumstances.

Elizabeth Weil writes eloquently of such a place for her, a park across the street from the home where she grew up:

> For chronic movers like me, and for the hectic lives that we all seem to live, there's no balm quite like that of returning to the same physical spot again and again while the world rushes by at breakneck speed. These places become touchstones, geographic constants to repair to year after year, and sanctuaries to which to retreat when not much else makes sense. T.S. Eliot referred to such places as "the still point of the turning world," the deeply meditative spots "where past and future are gathered," and where our lives seem most clear. For me the clarity of geographic touchstones has provided joy, solace, a much needed wake-up call, hope in times of despair, lucidity in times of confusion, an overbearing need to tell my barely cognitive two-year-old about my childhood, and even a sweet form of regret. These touchstones are sentimental, sure, but in the best possible sense. They are landscapes we have soaked in memory; they are walk-through scrapbooks of our lives.[1]

One such "geographic touchstone" in my life is a hundred-year-old cabin on a lake surrounded by mountains in Colorado. I can glance at the photos placed about and see my grandparents walking up the road with fly rods, Grandpa in a red plaid flannel shirt and Nana in a jaunty blue dress, holding a handsome trout; my parents, dating at the time, on horseback wearing tall riding boots; and my sons in clothes spattered with mud from mountain biking. A childhood family lineup on the lakeshore including my brothers, my cousins, and me goes boy, boy, boy, girl, boy, boy, boy. Would you guess that I was spoiled?

It is a place soaked in family memories. Not all of them are good memories, of course. But it is hallowed ground where they come flooding back so easily and where it is natural to think to tell my sons about the time, for example, that we made Uncle David into the Jolly Green Giant for a floating boat parade by mixing Noxzema and green food coloring and smearing it on him—and then it wouldn't come off. And to make matters worse, he's red-green color blind and couldn't find where to scrub.

Author Nessa Rapoport remembers such a place in her memoir *House on the River*: "Hearing the rain on the roof above us, I am inhabited by a very old feeling of sanctuary, of sitting with my grandmother on the porch, the unsynchronized turning of our pages the only sound beyond the rain that speckled the screens, while a bouquet of water, sodden wood, and drenched leaves rose from the river."[2]

These sorts of memories, layered year by year through generations, make a place unmistakably home.

Home as a Stable Place

Kurt says, "If I was ever to call anyplace home, it would be the ranch [owned by his great-grandfather and now his grandfather]. Why? Because it has the continuity from all the way past to now. All the memories and all the everything is kind of contained there, so it's the place you feel the most history." The ranch represents family history condensed in one place over decades.

Sara mourns the loss of this sort of stability from the home where she grew up: "Until I was eighteen I lived in the same house. Then my parents divorced and sold the house. I just miss that house so much. I miss that I can't show my husband the house I grew up in. For me home is definitely that house. When I feel really alone or overwhelmed or I'm lying in my bed at night, I'll go through my old house in my mind. I just go through living there and growing up there. . . . I think the key is *stability*." That's the word for Kurt's family's ranch too.

A few months after Hurricane Katrina, a woman named Yvonne kept coming back to her damaged home and climbing upstairs to her bedroom, which wasn't damaged, just to take a nap. Just being back in the stability of her own home, in her own bed, was comforting to her.

Lori, on the other hand, wonders at times why she's not more drawn to one place. "In literature there's this big thing right now about place and the significance of place and choosing to anchor yourself to a place because of the growth that comes from it—how we develop as humans when we stay rooted. I've been reading a lot and feeling really torn because I don't have that experience. By the time I got married I'd lived in over twenty different houses. We've lived in Grand Rapids almost six years, but we don't want to spend the rest of our lives there, and that keeps you from putting down roots, even though I'm seeing that that's something I'd like to value. So I've been actually starting to try to look for some books by people who have some other experiences."

Lori thrives on change. "There is nothing in the world that gives me more energy than doing something new," she says. "Being somewhere new. I just love it. And so I'm fed by the opposite of stability, which is really odd. The struggle for me is life isn't always [providing new experiences]. Like in Grand Rapids where life is the same every day. How do I adjust to that?"

"We have the opportunity to travel internationally," Lori continues, "so we don't choose a second home because that would keep us from all this other opportunity." She admitted, though, as she thought about it, that her family does camp all the time at the same site. The campsite is close to Lake Michigan, with no outhouse or facilities, and her kids came up with a name for it: Home Sweet Home.

Many people find some experience of stability of home important, while others are stimulated by a variety of different places, but ultimately everyone longs for someplace they can call home.

Nebraskan or Floridian?

For some people the fixed spot on the map that means home is a larger circle. It encompasses a state or region, even a country. Regional authors like Kathleen Norris in the Dakotas, Eudora Welty in Mississippi, or Wallace Stegner in the arid West must feel a kinship with their region that drives far down into their DNA.[3]

Kelly lived and worked in both Burkina Faso and Indonesia, and each time she came "home" to the United States, she experienced a welcomed letting down, a shedding of the constant need to be "on" in another culture, to be always aware of what she was wearing or saying. The long, quiet flights were a bridge for her out of life in Indonesia back to being with people she blended in with. She didn't have to worry about saying things in a particular order or being careful to honor the right person first. In such ways our country is home to us.

In *The No. 1 Ladies' Detective Agency*, Obed Ramotswe, father of the main character, expresses it like this:

> But why should I want to go to Zululand? . . . I said to him that Zululand sounded fine, but that every man has a map in his heart

of his own country and that the heart will never allow you to forget this map. I told him that in Botswana we did not have the green hills that he had in his place, nor the sea, but we had the Kalahari and land that stretched farther than one could imagine. I told him that if a man is born in a dry place, then although he may dream of rain, he does not want too much, and that he will not mind the sun that beats down and down. So I never went with him to Zululand and I never saw the sea, ever. But that has not made me unhappy, not once.[4]

What map do you have in your heart? It might be of a state or an area that people would think you're crazy to claim. Another home in my heart is Kansas. I have lived in Colorado for nearly all of my adult life. And let's face it, which of these two states would you prefer as home? On the surface anyway. Yet if you asked me what state I called home, I would tell you Kansas. I agree with Obed Ramotswe. I have a map of prairie in my heart.

Your Home's Relationship with Nature

Whether or not you currently live in your "geography of home," your natural environment influences your experience of home. It lends a pervasive mood, for one thing. Either you like and are stimulated and brightened just by being in the environs of your home, or you might be disappointed or feel your mood dampened by one good look around. If the latter is the case, what elements can you control that would bring a brighter prospect? If there's not much you can do, you can still bend your own attitude to find the beauty that is there but hidden.

Nature gives us free gulps of beauty. We want to guzzle all the beauty we can in the space we call home. We want to encourage, enhance, and enjoy it where we can.

Windows allow a home to inhale and to exhale. Living in a climate that's conducive to having windows open much of the year, I now feel stifled and claustrophobic when they're closed. Windows let in not only breezes and fresh air but also life sounds that connect us with the natural world. Even traffic sounds connect us with larger life.

A window can also serve as a movie screen. Barb makes family entertainment of a rip-roaring thunderstorm, partly to dispel her children's fear of it. They sit on the sofa watching the storm out the picture window, eating popcorn and drinking ice cream floats.

Kathy and Tom chose their home for its views and its porches. They have a big porch outfitted with a copper fireplace, sky chairs that hang from the ceiling, and four rockers. When it's not too windy, they eat out there.

Cathy's house is bulging with a large family, and it's hard to keep the place clean. But one real source of beauty for her was a pond her son dug in the backyard. They stocked it with fish, which her daughter named, and Cathy planted flowers around it and placed benches for sitting and observing it all. This became a spot for quiet conversation (in a household of nine) and prayer.

Cathy and her fish-naming daughter were distraught when the son who dug and maintained the pond went through a hard time and neglected the pond—and over the winter the fish froze. In the spring the pond began to stink.

When they dug out the pond liner and put it in the trash—behold! Underneath was sand that the grandkids quickly claimed. Now it's the favorite spot again! All the kids gather in the sandbox, and the great-grandparents have a ringside seat on the bench. Does your property have a stinking pond that could become a happy sandbox?

Rebecca thought that she and her husband needed to bring nature into their urban apartment, so she bought a grill for the deck and a few pots for plants. But she found that the plants "crisp up in no time" because it's so hot and dry. "We both enjoy

PLANTING AND MAINTAINING A CUTTING GARDEN

Carla enjoys the beauty and the creative process of working in her garden of flowers that she will cut and enjoy inside. Of course gardens aren't always beautiful. Gardening also means weeds and work. Here are some of Carla's gardening tips:

Be patient and consider your garden a work in process.

Study what plants thrive in your climate by observing neighbors' gardens and local nurseries. You'll have your best chance of success with these.

Try a mix of perennials (that come back year after year) and annuals (that you must plant again each year). Choose colors you enjoy.

Plan your garden so that when one flower finishes blooming, another flower begins to bloom.

Notice what flowers work well and you really enjoy, and plan to make changes for next year so that your garden includes more of those.

Don't be intimidated by the job of keeping up your garden. Carla makes one little spot look great at a time, then turns her attention to another spot. She says, "I do this ten-minutes thing. We grill most nights in the summer, and I'm the griller. I put the chicken or fish on the grill and take my little weeder and weed where I can see the grill. When the food's done, I've got a six-foot section weeded!"

[nature], but we don't feel like we need to own it," she says. "We'll go to the park and that's fine. I like watching people, seeing other people. We didn't have that when we had a backyard. I don't miss the yard."

Even commuting can let us receive from nature as we approach home. "We live in the foothills," says Stephanie R. "As soon as I start driving into the neighborhood, I'm going home. There's a buildup. Our setting, the outdoors, does play a big part."

Sharman and Bob move a lot, and they have a tradition of always planting lilac bushes at their new home. "It's a nostalgic thing for us," says Sharman.

Becca and her kids take advantage of their patio to plant a pizza garden in pots. They plant tomatoes, oregano, and other things that they like on pizzas. So gardening and cooking together are all part of the experience.

Then there's the beauty that's up for grabs if we'll just take our blinders off and see it surrounding our homes. Like sunrises and sunsets. If you're not up for the sunrises, you ought to at least catch the sunsets. I like to try to name what the sunrise's colors might be in a big Crayola set. You might find other descriptions. There are a particular dusty grey and dusty brown in our Colorado sunrises that are just like the colors of Necco wafers. Exactly.

G. K. Chesterton said that the sunrise is like God saying, "Do it again!" to the sun, and the sunset is like God saying, "Do it again!" to the moon. So did you think yesterday was great? Well, let's do it again! Or today wasn't so great? No problem, we'll try it again tomorrow! Each day is a fresh chance.

Kathy D.'s family lives on a farm and ranch in western Nebraska, and this life provides a particular closeness to nature. "When you bale alfalfa at three or four in the morning, you see the world wake up," she says. "The sky does a hundred things before the world wakes up. The sunrise is never the same."

Heidi and Amy from Australia love the bush that surrounds their home, the birds like kookaburras, galahs, and lorikeets, and even the lizards and iguanas. "They're all around us because the bush is all around us," they say. "It's so relaxing."

Does your home echo with the sound of cicadas on a summer night? Does the rain scour your streets and sidewalks and afterward make the whole world smell new? Have you ever sat on the stoop and watched a mother bird teach her baby to fly, hopping up the tree trunk with him, then shooshing him out the limb and off to flutter down with Momma right behind? The natural environment can add so much to the simple pleasure we find in our homes.

At Home with the Weather

At its most basic level, a home is a shelter from the elements, whether the home is under a bridge or in a yurt. In fact, we rarely appreciate our homes more than when they buffer us from extremes: air conditioning when it's one hundred degrees outside, a humming furnace when it's minus-twelve.

In Colorado the climate is more temperate than most non-Coloradans imagine, but we have occasional blizzards that bring all transportation and commerce to a halt with a barricade of white.

During our last spring blizzard, the kids and a couple of their friends gathered at our house on the evening the storm began, knowing a couple of feet of snow had been predicted. There's nothing like a good snowstorm to draw you to hibernate with others. Cabin Fever when alone is much worse—and scarier—than Cabin Fever shared (well, unless it's shared with toddlers).

So we had bodies in all beds and on the sofas, warm and snug as the wind howled and snow fell. At such times I feel like a mother hen gathering her chicks safely under her. I love to go to sleep knowing that the house is full and everyone's needs are met.

The next day we all played cards and games at the kitchen table by the fireplace and ate anything and everything that was in the house. By midafternoon the kitchen chairs were cramping and curiosity got the best of us. We bundled up and ventured out to see how far we could sink into the snow, to shake snow off burdened tree limbs, and to begin shoveling the driveway, taking frequent breaks to complain with shoveling neighbors about how hard it was to shovel the driveway, and to cheer on the neighbor who worked his way down our sidewalk with a snowblower.

Yes, homes are at their peak of performance when they protect us from extreme elements.

Kathy D. loves the pace of life on a farm or ranch, which she says is "a combination of what we personally set for ourselves and what Mother Nature does." Much of her family's daily pace is set by what they must try to get done before that cloud erupts or the wind comes up. They spend a good deal of time on the land, which can dish out great extremes: blizzards to scalding heat to driving winds. These are things over which they have no control.

But their life also includes an internal pace they set for themselves when they are in their home. Kathy fondly talks about their "camping spots" in the family room. She and husband Bart and their two children each have their favorite spots. Dad's chair is always Dad's chair, where he reads the paper. Alyssa's chair has her crocheting by it. Next to Kathy's chair is a pile of books. Kathy loves to relax when she comes inside: "I like to have a glass of cold iced tea or water. I can read the paper. Things don't have to be done immediately."

Nature has both beauty and a fearsome side that it displays through extremes of weather and natural disasters. As a child, when the tornado sirens wailed—which seemed to happen pretty regularly on early summer evenings—I took my favorite doll and sat in the southwest corner of the basement with my family (except my father, who loved to stand outside and watch the clouds), listening to the crackling voice on the radio tracking the path of the storm. I distinctly remember the sensation that we had no control over what was happening and what it felt like not to know whether there would be a house above us when it was over.

I'm sure that tornadoes helped shape my concepts of God and man—how puny we are and yet at the same time how precious we are to him. In times of disaster, how we'll accessorize the family room and whether we need to change the furnace filter are stripped from our consciousness as we get down to what is really important. Afterward, when the dust settles, we look back on these times as bittersweet because they snap us out of the trivial and remind us of the important. They remind us of our need for the dependable shelter of home.

Celebrating the Seasons

It's fun to bring the bounty, colors, and changing moods of the seasons into our homes.

Kathy keeps labeled totes in her basement holding commemorative stashes for each season and holiday: Fourth of July, fall, Christmas, winter, Valentine's Day, St. Patrick's Day, and Easter. Kathy's four-year-old nephew, Wayne, was visiting on St. Patrick's Day and got snowed in for an extended stay. He was fascinated with Kathy's leprechauns displayed all about, so she decided to bring up the Easter totes and let Wayne help her decorate for the next season.

This was all new to Wayne, and he had definite ideas as to where each item should be placed. In particular he believed that the statue of Jesus praying in the Garden of Gethsemane needed to have his own Easter bunny nearby. Wayne combined her collection of crosses with Easter eggs. "It was a huge memory for him," said Kathy, "and a huge memory for me to have done it with him." She felt it was important to leave Wayne's odd arrangements after he left. He gave her family a fresh view of Easter.

Lori's family celebrates the first snow each winter by making homemade donuts and frosting them with a combination of Baileys Irish Cream and powdered sugar. Friends call them on the first snow to see if they can come over.

In Claire's home the kitchen counter is the center of seasonal decoration. It is a flat, smooth surface that is the family hub for homework and projects. "When you get up on your birthday, the area is covered with streamers and banners, and there are presents at your place. For Valentine's Day the area is covered with little white lights. If a child receives a great report card, on the kitchen counter is a coupon for an ice cream cone. The kitchen counter is our main event," says Claire. She doesn't need to decorate the whole house. This one area, central to family life, will do.

For some of us, the home of our heart is a place associated with way-back family memories and stability. For all of us, the beauty and unpredictability of nature and changing seasons can enrich the surroundings and our experience of home.

Home Tour: Facts of Life on the Farm

On the farm Kathy D.'s kids see the life cycle: birth and death, planting and harvest, forces beyond their control. "We get lots of opportunity to witness God's hand. Lots of times the details make you say 'Wow!'" It leads to a lot of what Kathy's kids call "Mom's little sermons."

Actually her "sermons" are prompted by the kids' questions: Why did that calf have to die? Why did we have that storm? How did the calf get in there? Why does it have to come out *there*?

"*Being born, dying* are not just vague words to our kids," Kathy says. Living in the country, "they've seen them [animals] be born, and they know what a miracle that is. They are savvy to the beauty of it."

Their kids—Chase, ten, and Alyssa, nearly fourteen—understand well the power behind natural forces, and they are sympathetic to people dealing with natural disasters. Kathy shares with her kids requests that she's received for prayers for those facing forest fires in Arizona and floods in the Northeast, because she knows their compassion. And, she says, "They make for good family conversation."

Reaching Outside

Part 2

8

Generations, Celebrations, and the Changing Nest

When Dan and Stephanie became engaged, Alex and I rose quickly to our parents-of-the-groom duties and asked where they would like to hold the rehearsal dinner. They decided they wanted to go to a place where the evening could be open-ended so they could hang out with family and friends who had come from far away. And they wanted some activity besides eating. So we checked out a few places with them, after which they came to us and said, "We want it in your backyard."

This was not what I had envisioned. I wanted to go to a restaurant where I could engage with the people and the exciting event with no responsibility besides paying the bill. But on the night of the dinner, as I stood back and watched the caterer set up and serve a festive, delicious Mexican dinner (casual, colorful, inexpensive—I heartily recommend it) and family from both sides blend at round tables spread around the lawn; as I watched games of croquet and bocce ball; as dusk softened the scene and candles flickered warmly on each table—I understood.

Home is the base for gatherings that provide the continuity of family. It is where we celebrate the mix of everyday times and special celebrations that shape our sense of identity as a family and our heritage or traditions and values. Home is where family happens, generation after generation.

Mixing of Generations

The combining of several generations creates a rich gumbo. Sometimes it's fiery; sometimes it's bland. Usually a few strange lumps are folded in that enrich the flavor if they are present in moderation. American families are often handicapped because they don't have as many "ingredients" living near them to simmer together. We have to make the most of fewer times of mixing or find local replacements for the in-between times.

I remember what a joy it was to have Alex's great-aunt Dorothy visit from California. All she wanted to do each day was sit at the kitchen table and color and play games with the boys. And it's a treat to have our niece Diane come over for the weekend and wonder that she can play by the hour with my purses and shoes.

Each summer Jennifer takes her four children to her mother's beach home on Lake Huron in Canada. Her sisters and their children inhabit the cottages on either side of their mom's place. Each morning the sisters join their mother on the porch of her cottage for tea. Tea may last for two hours as the sun rises over the lake and the kids slowly wake up and help themselves to cereal. This summer Jennifer was overwhelmed with thankfulness for what she has there. She feels she's taken the beauty of it for granted for much too long.

A grandparent's home is generally the breeding ground of lifelong sensory memories. Do you remember visiting your grandparents' home? If you close your eyes and think about it, I'll bet your senses can take you there: taste, touch, sight, sound, and particularly smell. Sometimes the memories are strangely random. My grandfather seemed to be always back in a little den, either at his typewriter or lying on a daybed listening to baseball games. I hear a sportscaster on the crackly radio and taste the odd, bitter horehound candy he would offer me from a jar on top of a bookcase. Who knows what memories our children will have of our parents' homes or their aunts' and uncles' homes. Whatever their senses discover there will enrich their experience of the combination of environment and relationships that create home.

Some of these places may be haunted houses: haunted in the sense of enclosing troubling behaviors, past or present. Our memories are conflicted; our reactions are tough to untangle. Mother-daughter relationships, for example, are not always so idyllic. Stephanie observed that most of the women in her Bible study group had difficult relationships with their mothers. They don't want to repeat the cycle with their own children, so they talk about what they can do with their children in their own homes to be "good moms." We aren't responsible for these haunted places. We're only responsible for our own homes and for the values that shape our choices there.

Home as a Stage for Holidays

Holidays and celebrations like anniversaries, baptisms, and birthdays mark a pause in the day-to-day to commemorate something of importance to us. Our homes provide the very best venues for these events. We can decide the time, how long it will last, the guest list, the refreshments, the program, the decor, the degree of formality, and most importantly the privacy. Such a deal! As a bonus we are creating layers of good memories of milestone events in our homes. There are times, of course, when we may choose to hold an event elsewhere. But the default for celebrations and holidays is at home.

When celebrations are at home, they can stretch our home's resources but also can show them at their shining best. Planning a celebration involves striking a balance between the environment you want to provide, the size and scope of your resources, and the number of people you want to invite. Chrissy loves to entertain and couldn't wait to invite her whole extended family over the first Christmas that she and her husband owned a home. They had a small table and four chairs, so Chrissy bought an eight-foot collapsible table and put it in the living room. But the table filled the room and squished the people uncomfortably together. She learned, however, and the next summer she hosted a family barbecue in their more spacious backyard.

Steve and Jennifer and their four children go to Kansas to stay with his parents each Christmas. Steve's brother and family—eight of them—stay there too. The grandparents have developed strategies to make this workable and fun. They vacate the master bedroom for a smaller guest bedroom upstairs, leaving Steve and Jennifer in the master bedroom with their kids on the floor in sleeping bags. The family of eight has a similar arrangement in another large bedroom.

At least one night Grandma and the granddaughters have a sleepover in the basement. They eat popcorn and watch movies, and Grandma sleeps on the sofa while the girls encircle her in sleeping bags. Grandpa and the boys have their sleepover time too, with Grandpa on a foam mattress on the floor.

Fourteen-year-old Alicia creates videos of all the cousins to commemorate these special holidays. She creates short scripts for each child to read or act out for the camera. Then after Christmas she mixes this footage with still photos from the holidays and creates a DVD for each family member.

At our home one Christmastime we wanted to create an evening that encouraged lots of cross-generational family interaction. We set up three "stations": cookie decorating and baking in the kitchen, Chinese checkers in the dining room (all ages could play), and making a craft by sticking whole cloves in an orange in the breakfast room. All family members had to rotate

HOME BIRTHDAY PARTIES, RADIC STYLE

Shelly Radic used to think a birthday celebration had to be an over-the-top party that she spent weeks planning and presenting, ending up "like a maniac. I was so focused on the party that I wasn't celebrating my kids."

When Shelly realized this, she made a conscious change. "When I switched my focus over to celebrating the child, the parties were much simpler," says Shelly, "but they were still as much fun. The kids still had a great time. And I was more relaxed, so I could enjoy my own kids." Here is Shelly's basic plan:

- Each child has a birthday party every other year.
- The off-party year is focused on special family time for the child with grandparents and cousins.
- One or both parents write a birthday letter to the child, sharing what they love about him, how he's grown, or where they imagine him going in the next year.
- The birthday party's theme is something the child particularly likes: a dinosaur party, a tea party, a ballerina party. Some of the decorations can be taken from items you already have at home.
- Set a realistic budget.
- Let the child choose the menu.
- Invite the number of guests of the birthday child's age plus one.
- Enlist a helper for every four guests, with a two-adult minimum.
- Plan at least two or three more activities than you think you'll have time for and vary their pace: quiet activities interspersed with more rambunctious games.

to two of the three stations during the evening. It was a rousing success!

These attempts are not always rousing successes, but in general a little imagination in the use of resources and a dash of surprise to get people out of their ruts are recipes for success.

One thing I love about these gatherings is what I like to call tableaus, which are like freeze-frame snapshots of a poignant sight. I savor the sight of Grandpa and a teenage son laughing over a game or a granddaughter helping Grandma tie a ribbon around her orange. Your home in many ways is a catalyst for these connections, over and over again.

Over the long term, the events that don't go just perfectly often become the ones the family reminisces about together time and again. On Thanksgiving, my favorite holiday, Alex and I cook dueling turkeys. He barbecues his on the Weber grill, and I cook mine in the oven. Invariably mine turns out golden and succulent, magazine perfect. His turns out charred and shriveled—and everyone likes his best.

One Thanksgiving the usual congregation of people was chatting in the kitchen amid warmth and good nibbles and smells. Alex's turkey was done (very done), and he had removed the grate with the turkey still on it and propped it on two bricks on the grass to cool.

We kitchen chatterers glanced out the window just in time to see our standard poodle, Gus, bounding across the yard, dragging the turkey by one leg. The turkey was rescued, and after a few minutes of debate we discarded the leg, carved the turkey, and ate it. This turkey was so much more memorable than any of my golden birds.

For the major holidays—Thanksgiving, Christmas, and Easter—our homes themselves and the very bustle in them that gets wearing to us are a precious asset. People who live alone or who live with a quiet few, but not necessarily by choice, may envy what they imagine is happening inside your walls. Perhaps you can invite someone into the inner circle of your holiday. Shari and Dave know a single woman from Uganda, and they invite her to stay with them for a couple of nights at Christmas to get the full effect. This is a beautiful expression of this family's thankfulness for the home that they can enjoy and share.

Why We Celebrate as We Do

What are the values we embrace as we approach a celebration? What is the holiday's significance, and what will make it meaningful to us? What are nonnegotiables in the way we celebrate special events in our homes?

With these sorts of questions we form the values surrounding our family celebrations. They'll be tested sometimes, and it's helpful to have discussed and resolved them ahead of time.

Rebecca and Nathan live in a loft apartment in the city that not only doesn't have a guest room but also has very few interior walls that reach clear to the ceiling. It is not possible to carry on a private conversation there.

When they bought the loft, they talked about their families and holidays, since all their extended family members live out of town. They decided that for the cost of what it would take to buy a loft with an additional bedroom, they could put a family up in a hotel when they came to visit. For some of their family, that was a contrary thing. But Rebecca and Nathan decided it was important to do what made sense for 360 days of the year rather than for the three or four days that they would have company.

In our family we found a plan that works for the "where, when, and with whom shall we celebrate Christmas" decision that most families jockey with until they find a workable scenario. Alex's family were Christmas Eve people from way back. Alex's Grandma Lagerborg served the traditional Swedish lutefisk on Christmas Eve, and then they opened presents. However, in the next generation, Alex's parents brought to this tradition a preference for dining slowly and late. The last time we participated, we took our three little boys to his parents' home for Christmas Eve. We began eating dinner at 8:30 p.m. and began opening presents at 10:00 p.m. We pulled into our garage at midnight with three children crying because they were so tired. Alex and I agreed that this was not the Christmas Eve memory that we wanted to establish for our children. Plus, our church's Christmas service was on Christmas Eve, and we didn't want to miss it.

The next Christmas we told his parents that we would be going to church on Christmas Eve and that they were invited to our home on Christmas morning to open presents and to have Christmas dinner at noon. This was not a popular announcement. It flew in the face of two generations of family tradition. But it wasn't working for us.

Sometimes those boundaries need to be drawn and maintained. Debate generally doesn't help. In our case the furor didn't subside for three or four years, and our decision was tested each Christmas season. But we held firm, extending the invitation for dinner on Christmas Day, and now a new tradition is comfortably in place.

The lutefisk tradition, however, has wavered. As often happens, one family member, Alex's grandmother, a first-generation Swedish American, made it faithfully every year. She would soak the fish in lye, then cook it in a rice pudding over which she poured white sauce. The lutefisk was a ceremonial first course to Christmas dinner. With it we passed the pepper grinder and covered the top with black sprinkles to mask the fish taste while kicking over the blandness. While eating the lutefisk we evaluated how it tasted this year as compared to last year and whatever year was currently considered the best year.

When Grandma L. passed away, Alex's father inherited the sacred preparation of the lutefisk (he used frozen cod). When he passed away, Alex's brother took it on for a while, but the fact was that nearly all the avid lutefisk lovers had died. Do you continue a tradition like that, and stink up the kitchen on Christmas morning cooking it, just because it's your heritage? Should Melinda keep preparing her mother's Mexican tamales? Should Kathy make her mom's Bohemian potato dumplings and sauerkraut?

In our case, after a few years' disappearance, the lutefisk has made a comeback. I think it's because we didn't latch on to any other family signature dish. There's something to be said for a tradition that sets you apart as a family, even if it's because you love to complain about it. And the smell from the kitchen on Christmas morning? It is at least our special smell. It is the smell of Christmas with family at home.

Beth's husband Rob was in the military, and as they've spent Christmas living in many places, they've experienced a variety of other families' holiday traditions. "I hear about new traditions and I think, *Why didn't I start that ten years ago?*" says Beth. "But I tell myself, I didn't know about it ten years ago, but now I do, and I can start doing it now!"

Creating Home Somewhere Else

For Beth and Rob, for twenty years home was where the military sent them, including to Turkey. Beth said, "Our first Christmas there we were hanging the ornaments on the tree and realized that this was home, because this was where we were celebrating birthdays, holidays, and special occasions. And I never would have thought that a military base in Turkey would be home. It was where I loved my kids and made the family dinners and tucked them in at night. So it became home even if it wasn't what I was dreaming of."

A friend who was helping her elderly mother move to a retirement home commented on her mother's difficult transition, "So much of who you are is in your home." It's often hard to uproot to a new home and create a new sense of who you are as influenced by your new home.

Carla's family reached a point where their home felt too cramped for their four family members and they needed to move. But at the same time Carla was grieving the death of her mother, and her garden and an enormous tree over the deck were comforting to her and made it hard for her to leave. Providentially, a storm split the tree in half so that they had to have it removed. After that it was okay for Carla to move on to another house and another garden. But we have times in our lives when the familiarity and favoriteness of some aspects of home provide needed comfort and stability.

As Beth and Rob moved time after time, they developed patterns that made it easier on Beth and the kids. With each move Rob had a new job to report to, work to do, and connection with people. For Beth and the kids it was much harder. But the military network was an advantage. They often had a sponsor, a contact, waiting for them—someone who could tell them what housing was available and what living on the base was like. It helps to know as much as you can about the area to which you're moving.

Saying good-bye to friends is always hard, doubly so when you're having to watch your children say good-bye to their friends. "I learned that just because there was a geographic distance, a friendship didn't need to be over," said Beth. "So I developed a tradition. I never say good-bye; I always say, 'I love you and I will see you as soon as I can see you.'" She also expressed to Rob early on how important it was for her to stay connected with her friends by phone. "Just because we move, I don't want to lose my friends," she said, "so we may always have a huge phone bill." Rob answered, "Okay, I hear that."

Beth's first priority was always to get the kids connected and settled in a new home base. "Once they were reconnected and settled, whether that was in school or sports activities, and they were starting to make friendships, then I could take a deep breath and start to redefine what my life was going to be in the new location," Beth said.

Beth's family was rarely around their extended family, but on one particular move they adopted grandparents, the elderly couple next door. The couple grew particularly attached to daughter Katie Beth at a time when Katie Beth needed a little extra attention. The neighbor taught her to paint and told her how special she was, healing an ache in Katie Beth's heart. Adopted family are of the heart rather than of the blood, and they help round out the experience of what we can give and also receive in our homes.

The experience of moving frequently isn't necessarily a negative, according to Janie, Janice, and Mary, all of whom moved many times when they were growing up. Mary especially loved the experiences and remembers each home. "I play a game when I wake up in the middle of the night," Mary says. She calls the game "What house am I in?" She picks a time—say, when she was in the fourth grade—and she has to work her way back through all the houses she's lived in until she gets to that one. When she arrives back there in her mind, she imagines that home and says to herself, "That's where I am." Since she remembers each home so well, Mary's parents were probably intentional about creating a positive, if not permanent, sense of home.

The Changing Nest

In the life cycle of any family at home, the size of the household grows and shrinks as family members or even pets are born, grow up, launch out, and perhaps come back again. In our homes we continually prepare, welcome, and adjust to changes.

When Shari's son Charlie was born, daughters Cecilia and Caroline needed to share a bedroom. The girls' room was small, so they decided to put bunk beds in the center of the room with the headboard against a wall. They hung a curtain from the bottom of the upper bunk so that it enclosed the lower bunk. This gave the younger daughter Caroline privacy. The side of the room that her curtain opened up to was "her side," and the other side of the room was Cecilia's.

Meanwhile, Shari decorated the baby's room in neutral colors so she could have fun with accessories but the room wouldn't be too babyish for Charlie as he grew.

Beth's family faced a situation where Rob was working two

and a half hours away and they lived more apart than together for a year and a half. Although it was not what they wanted by any means, they carefully and prayerfully made the decision based upon the need to keep their two teenage daughters in their current school and social environment. They also had an older son away in college and a baby, Christa.

Rob lived in a basement apartment while he was at work. He drove there on Monday morning, home on Wednesday afternoon, back to work on Thursday morning, and home again on Friday night. His particular concern was to be as integral a part of Christa's life as possible, so he made it a point to get home on Wednesday night in time to rock her, tell her a story, and put her to bed.

"It was a very difficult time for all of us," said Beth. "It stripped our family to the bare foundations. We had to lean into everything we poured into the family for years before that." Family dinnertime was hard because they missed Rob and their son, so Beth and the girls often went to a restaurant for salads and good conversation. Beth got used to doing a number of things well, and when Rob came home he would wonder where he fit in. On the other hand, Beth had the advantage of their familiar home and routines.

One strategy that helped immeasurably was their "walkie talkies." In the evenings when Rob was home, they went for family walks in a beautiful area near their home. Then they'd come home and get the girls in bed before Rob and Beth went out walking again alone together.

Pam is living in a condominium following a divorce and the launching of her adult children. She reflects back on times when her family of four was together that she and her husband would get frustrated with the house as it was or would think, *If only the kids weren't in the house* or *If only we could have things that were new.* "But I always came back in my head to, *No, that's not what's important. What's important is having the kids at home . . .*

not the kind of house you live in. Suddenly I don't have all that . . . it's just me. It's not what I would have chosen. I'm trying to get used to the notion of having a house, being by myself, but not really wanting to be by myself." She says she is making the best of a bad situation by decorating as much as she can. "I love just being surrounded by things that make me feel good, whether they're from my past or they're colorful, because I love color. What is it that makes me feel good inside? I love being surrounded by pictures of my family. Pieces of artwork that remind me of places I've been. A little trinket I picked up in Ireland. Memories. Memories and color."

Janie and Bill have raised a blended family of six children, and Janie is surprised how much she is enjoying the empty nest. "This is the first time that we haven't had children around," says Janie. "We always had kids. We didn't have a honeymoon stage. Bill and I suddenly have to talk to each other. I thought I'd go through problems with the empty nest, but the phone isn't ringing off the wall. We have more things to talk about than you can shake a stick at. We could go off and have dinner. We could do what we wanted to do. We got pretty selfish with that, so now when the boys are home it's like, 'When are you leaving?' I enjoy having the kids home. They come home and visit. But it's just different."

Mary and Mert care for Mary's elderly mother in their home. "It's fine," Mary says, "but I do flip-flops between being in charge and being the daughter. . . . It's nice having someone to talk to who knows everything about your life, but it's also hard being the daughter." Constant caregiving had Mary tethered to the house. So she sat down with her two sisters, who live in town, and told them, "You guys can plan a trip to Greece and come to the table and just announce your trip. I haven't been to Park Meadows [a shopping mall] since Mother has lived with us because it's too far away." They came up with a plan whereby Mary and Mert would take a motor home to the mountains on weekends that were planned in advance and the sisters would take turns coming to the house to stay with their mother.

With the changing mix of generations and celebrations in our homes, we flex our home's resources, we set boundaries, and we make changes so that home can be the staging ground for the best of family times.

Home Tour: Johnson Family Productions

Sharon and Harold's basement is off-limits to the family's adults for several hours during extended family gatherings so the kids can prepare a surprise. To date they've conducted family talent shows, bowling, a carnival, a restaurant where the kids cooked the food, and family karaoke.

The talent show was particularly memorable, with acts by all ages. Grandpa played the harmonica (not well, his wife adds), a fifteen-year-old grandson performed magic tricks out of a suitcase, one dad juggled, another dad wrote and read a poem, an eleven-year-old granddaughter played the piano and sang, two four-year-olds sang frog songs together, and the youngest, a three-year-old granddaughter, demonstrated how she could button buttons!

Having Company

Early one Saturday morning Tim was leaving to drive to Copper Mountain ski area, where he teaches snowboarding on Saturdays. I stood in my bathrobe in front of the coffeepot, pouring a cup.

"Hey Mom, do you mind if I invite Steve home for dinner tonight?" Steve, he explained, was a ski instructor, a single guy in his midthirties.

"Sure. Know about when you'll be home?" I asked. Tim answered, then added as he went out the door, "Did I tell you? Steve used to be a chef." *Slam*.

For a few moments I was embarrassed over the dinner I had planned: meatloaf, mashed potatoes (more work than I usually go to, but a big hit), and green beans. Nothing fresh or nouveau. But knowing that there was no margin in the day for new choices, I went with it.

At around 6:00 p.m. I heard Tim and Steve come in the back door. From the kitchen I heard a sniff and Steve say, "Wow! It smells like a family."

This was a banner night for me because it released me. I understood that lots of people would love to eat a meal in our home, and it's actually an asset to smell, look, taste, and sound like a family. I lit candles on the table. Steve and the others thought the menu was just great.

Imperfect Is Better

We make having company a much bigger deal than it needs to be. It's often thought of as being in a stratosphere with either attending debutante balls or going to the dentist. The truth is, if you peel back the layers of expectations, you discover that a warm meal and good conversation are simple, valuable gifts that almost everybody enjoys. If you don't like to have company, probably either you didn't grow up having company in your home, or you don't think you are a good enough cook, or you don't think your home is "presentable"—or maybe all of these. Lack of time can be a legitimate excuse, but more often we use it as one when it's really not.

Put yourself in the shoes of the guest. Your family has been invited to some friends' home for dinner Saturday night. Do you really care what they're serving? Unless you're deathly allergic to something, probably not. You're just thankful that the work and the mess are theirs.

And when you walk into their home on Saturday, are you thinking, *Horrors! There are toys on the sofa. The bathroom sink needs wiping. I see crumbs on the kitchen floor along the counters*? Nope. You are celebrating these flaws because they validate your own humanity. You're thinking, *If she can invite us over and their house looks like this, then I could invite her over to my house and it would be all right.*

Same thing at the table. Do you care if they're serving tacos or pizza—or mac and cheese, for that matter? Of course not. This is fun! At worst it's an adventure.

Probably you offered to bring a dessert or a salad too. You were happy to offer because you felt badly thinking they would be going to all the work.

Now turn the tables. Those people coming in your door don't care what you're serving, and they're not going to be too picky about the atmosphere. Furthermore, your friend has probably offered to bring something.

I still pretzel up over this stuff. It's just in my nature to worry about it, but at least I can spot when I'm doing it and reason with myself. You may be either more relaxed or more uptight about having people over than your spouse or your roommate, and this takes some talking through and working a plan.

Two cautions that you will understand because you know people like this: First, no one enjoys being with a martyr. So if it's too much work, ask for help or streamline the plan so that you, your family, and your guests can enjoy the experience.

Second, don't apologize for everything. The food's cold. The dog needs brushing. There aren't enough chairs. When we apologize, we make people really uncomfortable for us, and they want to say "It's all right"—but they don't want to have to keep saying "It's all right." Trust that they will accept your imperfections and your home's.

Go with Your Strong Suits

Do you think homes have personalities? Cheerful. Gloomy. Cozy. Sophisticated. Dramatic. Peaceful. I've always sensed that the places we've lived in have had an atmosphere, a personality of their own. For example, we go to a mountain cabin every summer, and when the shutters are removed and we open it for the season, it's as if the place has been holding its breath until people come to fill it again with their laughter or quiet reflections. Its main feature is a porch looking out over a lake that draws people to pull up chairs and talk or dream alone with a cup of coffee.

Whether or not you sense personality in your place, your home does have its strong suits. And you should capitalize on these when

129

you have company. Perhaps it's a fireplace. Or a table that's just right for playing cards or board games. Or a cooktop on a kitchen island that people can stand around while you cook. Or a shade tree perfect for picnics. Or cozy seating with throws or comforters for watching movies. As you discover these assets of your home that people enjoy, play to these strong suits when you have company.

You also have strong suits when it comes to preparing meals for guests. If you enjoy cooking homemade soups, that's a good thing to serve to company; let them bring bread. Maybe you like to experiment with stir-frying or like to treat people to your grandmother's calzones. Maybe your ace in the hole is a deli down the street (no apologizing, remember?). Whatever works for you with little stress and that guests seem to enjoy is a strong suit that you should make use of often. The point is not the dish that's served but the attitude with which you serve it and the connecting that happens over it.

Becca is a thirtysomething mother of three and owner/chef of a catering business. She grew up with good, fresh foods and never gets tired of cooking and experimenting.

When Becca has company, it's usually other moms and their families, and she likes to stay within her style, her comfort level—not only in the food that's served but also in what her home looks like.

"The people I'll have over for dinner for the most part are all friends. We're all moms. We all work hard," she says. "First and foremost they're here because they love me. Not because they love my clean house. Not because they love that everything I do is perfect. We have people over because we love them and want to spend time with them. Today we just don't ever have enough opportunity to do that. . . . So stepping back and staying within your comfort zone is so important because you have so much more fun with people.

"Most of my friends really enjoy cooking," she continues. "We all like to try new things. We have kids, and we can't afford to go out all the time. With babysitters and all, that's a big night. So we cook together. The kids run around and play. We try something new. It's a great evening."

Like Becca, you might enjoy spending the day cooking for family or friends. Our friend Ramiro will spend all afternoon preparing his rellenos and green chili, and I don't feel guilty letting him do it because I know he loves the process. Amy expressed it well when I commented on the fact that she had worked all day on delicious Indian cuisine: "Yes, it was a lot of work. But it was my pleasure." If going to extra lengths on a meal is what you love, it's a strong suit. Go with it.

When people have gathered at your home for a meal, and everyone has cleaned their plates, and the presentation was attractive (lots of color), and you even had a good number of the food groups goin', and it wasn't stressful for you to prepare—keep track of that menu in a computer file or on a note card. That way you can remember what you put together and serve it again. Your guests won't know (unless your child tells them) that you served the same thing to other guests. You could do this with seasonal menus—a stew in the winter, fish to grill in the summer, and so on.

Guests of One Sort or Another

When we invite people into our homes, sometimes they are friends with whom we have a lot in common. Friends very much like us. Being in and out of each other's homes gives us the footing with each other, the knowing each other well, to forge strong, depend-on-each-other friendships. They come over frequently. We go over to their home a lot. Or maybe we just gather at one of the homes, but we don't keep score. We divide our joys and our sorrows with these friends. Life is better this way. But if we are only spending time with these friends, over time we become a more concentrated version of who we already are. If we remain in a small circle, we are affirming and not particularly challenging each other's bias and opinions and interests.

There are other people—lots of other people—we can invite into our homes who are not as much like we are, or so we think, anyway. But in many ways these people are the most fun because of the new directions they take us. The circle of our lives, experiences, curiosity, creative expression, and understanding deepen and expand.

One night an African American pastor, his wife, and their two daughters came to our Anglo home for dinner. At that time Drew was playing cornet in the grade school band. He was a beginner. Beginning an instrument is tough both for the learner and for the listener. Ken, the pastor, spotted the cornet case in the corner and asked who played it. He encouraged Drew to play for them, but fortunately Drew declined. Ken said he used to play the trumpet. He wondered how much it was the same.

With a little coaxing, Ken took that cornet to places it didn't know it could go. It's one thing to fill your home with recorded music. It's quite another thing to have a jazz musician bring lethargic brass to life! We come from different ethnic backgrounds, but through this performance and our shared conversation, Ken enriched our lives.

When children have the opportunity to get to know people of different ages, types of work, ethnicities, and religions in the safety of their home, they learn to converse with people easily, and they learn to move more easily into different living situations. They also gain a broader experience and understanding of humanity.

Consider a local college or university as a source of friends from other countries. Many students who will become leaders in their countries in law, business, government, or academia attend college, particularly graduate school, in the U.S. Studies show that few of these students ever set foot in an American home. How would the world be different if we were just more

THE WELL-STOCKED GUEST ROOM

Tissues

A lamp to read by

Flashlight or night-light

Alarm clock

Extra hangers in the closet (and room to hang something on them)

Bottled water by the bed

A fresh flower or some touch of beauty

Clean sheets

An extra blanket or throw

A few magazines of different types

A Bible

Pen and pad of paper

hospitable? And think of the rich experiences we could enjoy through these friendships.

When people are gathered in your home, one interesting way to get to know one another—no matter how long you've been friends or related—is to put a question on the table, as I mentioned in chapter 4. The formal way is to use place cards, each with a question written inside. Each person reads and answers his question. It should be one that has no right or wrong answer and for which anyone will have an answer, such as:

What is one way you've seen yourself grow this year?

What country outside the U.S. would you most like to visit?

What is a blessing in your life that took you by surprise?

The object isn't to make anyone uncomfortable, so one "rule" is that if you don't want to answer your own question, you can choose to answer someone else's. The other rule, most needed with kids, is that no answer is wrong or stupid.

Of course you can do this informally without the cards by simply asking everyone at the table to answer one such question. This is a great way to keep conversation from sliding into the same old, same old.

Sometimes company will come to stay in your home over a couple of nights or longer. Whether it's your best friend from high school or your mother-in-law, give yourself some space for taking a nap or running errands by yourself so that you can keep your own equilibrium and also keep the household functioning.

If someone comes to live with you for a while, it's important to be sure the situation is mutually healthy—for the family and for the guest. It's good to clearly communicate expectations: Will this person pay room and board? How much and when? What family chores will be their responsibility? What behavior is nonnegotiable in your home?

For several months a young man who was trying to figure out a new job path and resolve relationship issues lived in our basement. He had been a basketball player, and on summer nights we could hear him late at night dribbling and shooting baskets in the dark. *Thump, thump, swish. Thump, thump, swish.* Thinking things out. I'm sure some people thought us foolish to let him stay with us for so long. But we saw another side: he was mentoring our early teenage sons in positive ways. But the day came when it seemed clear that staying with us was prolonging his lack of commitment, and we had to ask him to move on.

When we open the door to guests, whether for a cup of coffee or an extended stay, invariably we enrich their lives—but especially we enrich our own.

Manners Matter

Good manners are a way to show respect to other people. But they also serve as a security blanket. It's embarrassing not knowing how to behave at someone else's table or at a restaurant with other people. And it's easier to learn manners at home than by being wrong or unsure in a social situation. When you boil it all down, there are four good manners to learn at home that will hold you in good stead—four biggies. The first one is to welcome guests with your attention. That may sound funny, but it makes a big difference to a person that you greet them at the door and not yell to them from the kitchen. It shows you've been looking forward to their arrival. Say good-bye in the same way. Do you know how it feels to have your host come out to the front porch, or even to the street, and wave you off? Very cool. It makes you feel special, and it's something so easy to do.

The second good manner is related to the first: offer guests something cold or hot to drink as they arrive, whether or not they've come for a meal. People relax better when their creature comforts are met.

Third, don't start eating until everyone is seated (unless it's a buffet) and a hot dish has been served to at least three or four people. This just shows respect for the other people at the table.

Finally, determine some sort of family signal for "FHB"— family hold back. This is important when it looks like there might not be enough food to go around and family members need to be alerted not to pile it on until guests have all they want. Maybe a quietly whispered "FHB" will work if they're within whispering range. Some sort of unobtrusive hand or eye signal might work better.

Having company can become a natural rhythm of life at home. It's simply sometimes including other people whom we want to get to know: people much like us, and also people who are interesting and different. A warm meal and good conversation are simple, valuable gifts both for the hosts and for the guests.

Home Tour: Sodas in the Basement Fridge

Rachel and her three roommates, all single women in their midtwenties, live in a suburban townhouse. "My roommates and I are very much family," says Rachel. "I don't have to be someone else at home."

This is intentional with these girls. They've worked at making their home feel family-like. One thing they do is to share their food. "We don't buy our own food. We share the food, and we each make a point of buying food regularly," Rachel says. "If you eat a lot of something someone else has bought, you might go to the store and replenish it. But it's not like 'this is my food.'"

Each of the women has decorated her own bedroom according to her own taste. But the basement family room, where they love to have company, was a joint effort in a western theme. They have brown couches that look leathery, pictures of cowboys hanging on the walls, and horseshoes and bridles around the room. Three of them had an old-fashioned western portrait taken, which is prominently displayed.

"It's a welcoming atmosphere," says Rachel. "Welcome to our home. Come in and be a part of our family. It's not 'Come in and be our guest.'"

"Help yourself" is the house rule for guests. The roommates keep a refrigerator in the basement stocked with sodas, in addition to drinks in the fridge in the kitchen. Sometimes guests help themselves to other items in the fridge that weren't meant for them . . . but oh well!

They keep the house clean but not immaculate. "It's not like you feel you're walking into a museum and you have to be really careful," says Rachel. "It's clean and welcoming, but it's still a home, and we want you to be part of it. I think people feel that way. We care about them, we're interested in them, and they are part of the family."

Home Tour: Christmas Dinner in Jordan

The expression "it's lonely at the top" can hold all the more true when the top people are living in a foreign country, far from family, friends, and their familiar culture. When Cal and Mimi Wilson were living in Amman, Jordan, on a project with USAID, they became friends with the American ambassador and his wife. So Cal and Mimi invited them over for dinner on Christmas Day.

They arrived with two cars—one armored car and one chase car—and four bodyguards who spent the day watching out front. Periodically Cal and Mimi took food out to serve to the guards on duty.

In addition, the Wilsons invited five of their own extended family members who were visiting in Amman and an Episcopal priest with his wife and four children.

The conversation piece of the day was a Christmas "tree" that Mimi fabricated out of eight six-foot poles. Since there are so few trees in Jordan, Mimi found these poles and set them up like a teepee in the living room. She wound strands of small white lights around them. The effect was stunning . . . if you were living in Jordan!

The guests each drew a number that corresponded to numbered places at the two tables so that people were randomly seated together and the children were shuffled in with the adults. This arrangement found the ambassador seated with the seven-year-old son of the priest, who hadn't a clue who the ambassador was but gamely worked at making conversation. And living in a social world where children were usually whisked away, the ambassador beamed with enjoyment of his dinner companion.

After a traditional turkey dinner, procured through the commissary, the guests changed from dressy Christmas dinner clothes to sweats, piled into cars, and drove to the desert for a walk. The ambassador and his wife chose to stay behind, and when the others returned, they were napping comfortably. Then, as the turkey carcass was boiled for turkey soup, the guests watched a movie.

And so they spent the whole day together—a treat when you're far from family on what can be a long, lonely Christmas Day. Mimi's expression for this kind of entertaining is, "Let's just be family." Lots of people at the top could use some "just being family" time—if anyone would just invite them.

At Home in Community

Morning after morning, Alex the early bird watched four neighbor women round the bend of our street, walking and chatting vigorously at 6:00 a.m. "You should ask them if you could join them," he told me a few too many times.

I debated. On the one hand, I needed the exercise, and I wanted to make friends in the neighborhood. We had lived in this house for ten years, and it bothered me that when an officer came to ask me what I knew about our next-door neighbor, who was being reviewed for a security clearance, I knew nothing, either juicy or boring, to report.

On the other hand, I wondered just how much Alex thought that I needed to walk off! And besides, what if they said no?

Finally I mustered up the courage to walk out of the house and join them one morning. And they said yes. Emphatically! It was the beginning of an early morning addiction. Truly, now I would think long and hard about moving out of the neighborhood because of how much I would miss this. Here's what I receive:

> six (it's growing) wacky neighborhood friends whom I wouldn't have gotten to know otherwise
>
> a time each day to process issues ranging from whether a neighbor should have painted his house a cocoa color to whether we should be at war

good exercise (what would I have weighed without this?)

reacquaintance with nature—full moons, sunrises, snowflakes, cooing mourning doves, an occasional wary little fox

the benefits of consistently rising early

acquaintance with John the Milkman and Danielle the Newspaper Delivery Woman

the real scoop on the best and worst neighborhood stores and services

the wonder of a little community that cares about my family, my home, and the environs of my home

The fact is that we enjoy each other, we're stretched by each other, and at times we need each other.

We used to live across the street from an elderly couple named Les and Olive. They lived in suburbia in a ranch-style home because they enjoyed having people of different ages, particularly children, around them. The proximity was so enriching for both our families that we made excuses to borrow things. We could have bought a card table and chairs for overflow dinner company, but it was more fun to borrow theirs.

When Les was cleaning leaves off his roof and fell off the ladder, we were there. When Drew particularly needed a home-baked oatmeal cookie, he knew Olive would have one. We needed each other in big ways and small. I felt badly that they had to look out their front windows at our unkempt yard, whereas we looked out at their immaculate one. But they didn't seem to mind a bit.

We miss out on so much when we stay huddled behind our protective double glass windows, uninvolved with one another.

Porches and Stoops

Front porches were a given on early American homes before air conditioning and cul-de-sacs with fenced yards and patios.

They're making a comeback, particularly in urban settings, because they help build community and coax people even cautiously out of their homes. More than half of new homes now sport front porches. According to the National Association of Homebuilders, 42 percent of new single-family homes had porches fourteen years ago. Now, it's up to 53 percent.[1]

When our boys were little, the front stoop of our home was a comfortable first step out of the house toward neighborliness. I could sit on the steps with a friend and talk while our kids rode Big Wheels up and down the sidewalk. I could remain semi-tethered to laundry in the dryer, to something in the oven, and to the phone.

Chuck has both a back patio and a front porch, and he prefers to sit out front. "In summer, I sit on my front patio, just watching. The neighbors call me [fondly] the neighborhood watchdog. I can see what's going on out front."

Ginger and her husband Dave chose to live in an older city neighborhood where porches are common. In a duplex up the street, Ginger says, "There's a . . . lady who's about sixty and . . . she's the nicest lady on the planet. She started talking to my dogs one day when I was walking them down the block." She noticed when Ginger was pregnant, and now she fusses over the baby every time Ginger pushes the stroller by her porch.

Where we vacation at a cabin in the mountains, many of the homes are owned by multiple generations of families. Next door the grandmother of the large family loves to sit on their front porch in a twig armchair, reading, watching the hummingbirds, and talking to family members who come and go. If I leave our house, heading down to the lake, inevitably Georgiana will call to me, "Hey, you, get over here!" She's kidding, of course, but when she calls, you don't dare walk off! You must sit a spell in another twig armchair, shooting the breeze. It's a cozy niche where time stands still and you could easily forget why you were even heading to the lake. This is what people have in mind, surely, when they build all those new front porches.

Intentional Neighborliness

The point is not the porch, patio, or stoop so much as a launching place to get us "exposed," out where we can relate to neighbors. It's one small step in being intentionally—or potentially—neighborly. Other steps can include purchasing gift wrap, pizza coupons, lemonade, and Girl Scout cookies from neighborhood kids. Sure, they're overpriced and you might never use the stuff, but someday it might be your own kids who are practicing salesmanship. Besides, these sales meetings on the front step can make for some good conversations.

But being intentionally neighborly can require much more—and reap deep benefits.

Ken tells about a friend he knew in Chicago, just a regular guy. But this guy's neighbors thought so highly of him and his kindness to them that when he died, they flew the flag in the neighborhood at half mast. Ken, who is a pastor, wonders in comparison what his neighbors would say about him. "I've asked the Lord, 'Help me to be a good neighbor.' That's more important than anything I do on Sunday."

What does it mean to Ken to be a good neighbor? "Be intentional about it. Take that extra step. Reach out. Get to know them. Let them get to know you. Be willing to be vulnerable. Don't come off as the perfect person. That scares people away. Show that you're a fellow struggler . . . we are cut from the same cloth." He continues, "Lots of us are wired to offer to help, but we're reluctant to take a neighbor up on help in return."

A rural community is an interesting study in how to be good neighbors.

"Our neighbors can live fifteen to twenty miles away," says Kathy D. When a neighbor gets hurt, everybody fills in doing whatever is needed: running cattle, harvesting, branding calves. She might wash a neighbor's clothes and leave one of her kids there to mow the yard. "This is typical to rural life. Generally generations of history go with it. That commitment is often historical. You're helping where someone helped your grandpa. In an urban community the people are more fluid. Roots are different—not that it's wrong."

Intentional neighborliness looks different according to its setting, but it is a significant step toward discovering the richness of relating to those around us.

Fluid Fences

In general, Liz loves raising her four children in a suburban neighborhood with lots of other kids. "I love that all our kids have to do is walk outside and in five minutes someone will be there. . . . I feel very blessed to live here. It's a great place for our kids.

"We have those neighbors that are so easy to be with," she continues. "They raise their kids like ours. It's fun to have them over. You can go borrow an egg. And then there are others who test the command to 'Love thy neighbor.' They're harder."

Life in the neighborhood can be perplexing. "I haven't really figured this one out, because I wanted to be the Kool-Aid mom," says Liz. "That's how I'd pictured it. The kids would come to play at my house. But if you don't have SEGA and PlayStation and don't get Batman cartoons, kids don't want to come play at your house. They'll ask, 'So, what PlayStation stuff have you got? None? Okay, bye-bye.'" Liz tries to walk a tightrope between what she and her husband think is best for their four kids and what neighbor families allow their kids to do. She tells her kids, "Every family's different, guys. What's important to them might not be important to us." So far her kids are all right with that answer. It's not a huge deal now. "But it's coming," Liz says, "and I hope I have it figured out when it does."

The important thing is that Liz realizes they don't have to succumb to neighbors' values. They can grapple with, form, and keep adapting their own.

Liz has a good relationship with most of the parents in the neighborhood, whether their values are similar or not. "We were at a picnic and a dad told me how he just loved our kids so much. How each child was so different and secure in themselves. I think there is mutual respect. We try and respect our neighbors. But there are others," she continues, "that the minute you turn your back they're speaking bad about you. And those you just smile at and wave to. Not that I avoid them, but I can't say I go out of my way to spend time with those folks. That's a downer. It's hard to spend time with them."

Julie is another mom who loves to have the neighborhood kids play at her house, and she struggles too: "I'm not sure I'm the person to give you advice, because I struggle with that daily—how to be nice and make the kids feel welcome but also have our own time as a family, because sometimes we need to close the door and have our own little respite place where it's just the four of us or just my kids [and me]. I have finally gotten to the point where I signal the older neighborhood kids. If the garage door is up, the house is open, and if the garage door is down, our house is closed. For the most part they respect that. It's usually open, but there are definitely days and times when our kids need a little quiet time, and we'll close the door."

Lisa has learned to set boundaries with the children next door. "We have these kids next door that my kids can't go out in our backyard without them coming over, and the language they use and the way they treat each other and the way they treat my kids is not appropriate. I put up with it for a couple of months. Then we got a new play set, and those kids were playing on it before our kids could, so I said, 'We're going to have a little family play time,' and they ran home, and I could hear them saying, 'She is so mean.' . . . I don't allow my kids to go over there. And if I have a problem with the kids, I send them home. . . . We're trying to have a healthy balance. You try to be welcoming and not judge, but I have to protect my nest."

How do you draw a line between two front yards? How do you keep your own children separated from other children, knowing that it is not the fault of the other children that they are being raised as they are? Can you make a positive difference in the neighbor child's life? Can you do it without causing lasting detriment to your own children—maybe even building character in them at the same time? It's tough. These moms are heroes to me, because they're doing the difficult work. They're not giving up in either direction.

We couldn't let our sons go play in certain homes. But we allowed neighborhood boys to play in our home, by our home's rules, if Alex or I were there. On a shelf I keep a small bear figurine that is hugging a ceramic Christmas package. This little bear is symbolic to me of these neighborhood struggles. It was given to me by a neighbor boy when he was about five or six. And although he gave this little gift with no explanation, I think he was saying, without knowing how to say it, "Thanks for hanging in with me. Thanks for giving me rules at your house. Thanks for letting me play here"—when it was very tempting to not let him play.

It can be a burden to have play centered at your home. But it's also a bridge, through the children, to getting to know your neighbors "where they live." And some of them just might be a great blessing to you.

Living in Community

Intentionally living in community is a significant step beyond neighborliness in connecting spokes from home to home. Kim and Bill chose to live with five families who were friends from church in a huge old house in the center of the city in intentional Christian community. When they began, three of the families had children, but Kim and Bill didn't. But twelve years later, when they moved out, they had Brandon, age nine, and Kayley, age five.

Each family had their own separate apartment, and then one apartment was the common space. They ate dinner together five nights a week, with one family taking meal prep each night. They took turns leading weekly meetings. And best of all, according to Kim, they hired an outside facilitator who came once a month to help them deal with difficult issues. Can you imagine how hard it would be for five families to decide (1) that the house needed painting, (2) whether they should do it themselves or hire someone else, and (3) what color to paint it?

"We discovered that community is messy and it's slow," says Kim. But looking at it from this side of the experience, Kim believes they learned valuable lessons. They grew as individuals because "when you're with a group of people like that, a community of people that holds you accountable, it pushes you to grow in areas that you wouldn't otherwise," says Kim. "We bring things from our families of origin that we don't even see. So there were things I had to look at in myself, that I had to be held accountable to by other people. It was hard, very painful at times, but I think I came away a stronger person. Now if I have an issue with someone or feel someone has an issue with me, I feel like I have the ability to talk with them. I can confront them directly, not in a bad way. I would say, 'I get the sense that you're upset with me about something. Have I done something to offend you?' I don't think I would have had that ability, because in my family of origin the pattern was if you're upset with someone, you talk to somebody else about it."

What does it mean to be involved in community—not necessarily living with four other families like Kim and Bill, but to be in very intentional relationships? What forces propel us toward community, in counterbalance to the more comfortable, safe motives that draw us in to close our doors? "We four and no more," the expression goes. Why not simply revel in our capability to be quite self-sufficient in our well-provisioned, media-encased homes?

Pastor Rick McKinley says, "We are wired for community. Literally. Each of us has a belly button. Some are outies, some are innies, some are pierced. But we all carry this unmistakable sign that shows we were at one time physically connected to our mothers. Life begins for every human in utter dependence on another. But as we grow, our culture slowly sucks us into believing that we will truly be liberated only when we no longer need to depend on someone else."[2] What are some of our needs that are addressed by extending into community?

Why We Choose Community

Brandy's step into community was motivated by loneliness. While she was up in the night with insomnia during her pregnancy, she found a couple of online chat groups centered on her hobby of scrapbooking. She and her chat room friends shared ideas on how to organize scrapbook pages and new products. They shared digital photos of their work.

Now Brandy is involved in a multifaceted scrapbooking community. On the fourth Friday of the month, she has what she calls her "me" time. But it's very much "we" time, because at least one of her local scrapbooking friends comes along to a large scrapbooking store where they can crop to their hearts' content, sharing their stories as they do.

Patriotism has fueled Leona's involvement in local government on many levels. "For whatever reason, I had this sense of awe about the privilege of living in this country and felt it was part of responsible citizenship to stay involved," she says. She has served as mayor, on the water board, on the county planning commission, and on school committees, and she barely missed election to the state legislature.

In the midst of her political involvements, Leona maintains strong connections between community, family, and home. She loves to bake, so baking has become a strong home connection and has fostered several strong family traditions, like baking whole wheat bread. "I swear my children can smell it twenty miles away," she says. She has a Bosch bread maker and bakes six loaves at once. She's given the machines to all three sons, and they have all baked their own bread, but they prefer to come eat hers. Her two youngest granddaughters, who are preschoolers, are terrific little bread kneaders. And at Christmas she bakes thirty to forty loaves for neighbors and community friends.

Lee Ann knows her impetus for community is God-given. "When we lived in Mississippi, we visited a big city, and I saw some women working the street [as prostitutes], and it was one of those moments when the Spirit of God just crashes down on you. . . . I thought, *Those women are beautiful, and they don't know it. God has a plan for them, and they don't know it. If I ever get a chance, I want to tell them that.*"

When Lee Ann's family moved to Denver, she made good on this commitment. She started a day shelter to help women in prostitution come out of it. "Most of them have never had relationships with people who care about them unconditionally," Lee Ann says. "They've never had a functional home. So we help them experience community, family, a special place to be. We have a day shelter. It's pretty and beautiful and welcoming. . . . We want them to see themselves as worthwhile and valuable. God sees them that way." Lee Ann is committed to providing a loving home atmosphere.

Steve P. found that his church and small town community are literally his lifeline. A mountain-biking accident severed his spinal column, leaving him without the use of his body below his hands and arms. But he is able to live independently, in his own apartment, with the help of lots of community members. "There's probably seven other families here in the apartment complex that go to my church," says Steve. "When I need help, I can call my friends." He can also go out and ride his hand cycle

LEONA'S WHOLE WHEAT BREAD

(Makes approximately 5 loaves in 4 ½" x 8 ¼" pans.)

Blend together:

- 5 cups hot tap water
- 2/3 cup vegetable oil
- 2/3 cup honey
- 1 Tablespoon salt

Add 2 cups white flour and 4 cups whole wheat flour. Mix with dough hook or by hand.

Blend in 2 tablespoons granulated yeast. Add additional whole wheat flour to make stiff dough (usually about 5 additional cups).

Knead by hand or with dough hook. Let rise about 30 minutes. Divide into 5 loaves. Set into pans. Let rise another 30 minutes.

Preheat oven to 350 degrees. Bake for 30 minutes. Remove from oven and brush tops with butter or margarine. Enjoy!

Variations:

Cinnamon-Raisin Bread: Divide dough into 5 loaves. Roll out and spread with melted margarine or butter. Sprinkle with a mixture of brown sugar, cinnamon, and raisins. Roll up and place seam side down in pan.

Nut and Fruit Bread: Add 3 tablespoons sesame seeds, nuts, 1/2 cup sunflower seeds, 1 cup raisins or other dried fruit such as apricots or dates. You may wish to chop fruit into small pieces and coat with a bit of flour before adding to dough.

or his wheelchair in the parking lot and have the enjoyment of relating to the kids out there.

Is he lonely? "Sometimes," Steve says, "but I don't have to be." He has guys over for movie night once a week. They eat dinner, watch a movie, then talk about it together.

In Steve's small town, he can call the hardware store, and the manager will ring up what Steve needs and bring it out to his specially equipped van for him. He can go into the Safeway and be greeted with, "Hey, Steve, may I push the cart for you?" His pastor and church friends have stuck with him through it all. His community raised money so Steve could purchase his van. Steve's life would be much different without community. In fact, ironically, without community Steve would be more dependent, not less.

Extending the Home Safety Net to Community

It's true that sometimes fear of the unknown, of people unlike ourselves, and of the messiness and slowness of community will pull us away from community. But on the other hand, community can be a way to cast outward the safety net that is our home.

Kathy G. and Tom make community possible for the teenagers who are their children's friends. It's not unusual for Kathy to get a phone call like this: "Mrs. Adam's Mom, there's a bunch of us just hanging out here at Good Times Burgers. Can we come over?"

The kids know they are welcome. Kathy says, "My husband and I both welcome them with smiles. I think it started with my son's group of friends the summer that their class experienced three auto accidents. All of the five boys killed were from my son's class. After one of the memorial services, we encouraged Adam that the kids could come over. I was sitting on the front porch and I saw this long line of cars coming. I got up and just cheered. All that is to say we want them to feel welcome here, instead of being in a park doing who knows what."

Kathy and Tom learn the kids' names and ask them about what's going on in their lives. They hang out in the kitchen so they're available to the kids. The kids go downstairs, but Kathy's found they'll come up sometimes to talk. "What teenagers don't get today is respect," says Kathy. "They feel like they are being looked down on all the time. So we try to make our home a place where they find an adult who will engage and carry on a conversation with them. They love that! One girl came up to the kitchen and said, 'Thank you so much for making us feel welcome here. My mom would have told us to go home.'"

FOLLOWING QUILTS TO FREEDOM

Oral tradition maintains that one of the homiest of objects—the handmade quilt—was used to convey secret codes that moved escaped slaves safely along the safe-home network, a sort of community of escape, called the Underground Railroad. The stories maintain that there were ten quilt "code" patterns. Quilts were commonly aired out on fences, so the quilt with the appropriate pattern could be put out inconspicuously. When the "monkey wrench" quilt pattern was displayed, the slaves were to gather all the tools they might need on the journey to freedom. When the "tumbling boxes" pattern appeared on the fence, the slaves knew it was time to escape.[3]

The basement media room is furnished with garage sale furniture: two sofas, two loveseats, a big chair, and a pellet stove. They have video games and lots of old movies. A closet under the stairs is lined with board games.

Kathy and Tom have made boundaries clear through their own children. No sexual activity. No drugs, alcohol, or smoking. "My kids keep saying, 'They wouldn't do that here, Mom,'" says Kathy. "Since our kids were small, we've respected them: no belittling. We enjoy them and they enjoy us. We do a lot together. I think a lot of it is that we've respected them."

Sometimes our children's friends need this home safety net. And as we extend it, we hope that others will have their nets out when our children need extra covering. One night our phone rang shortly after midnight. Bad sign. The officer (another bad sign) asked me if I knew a young man named Jeff Johnson (not his real name). As my brain snapped awake, I realized that I did. He is a good friend of our son Tim.

Jeff was very drunk and was wandering in the middle of a major intersection. The officer was understanding. He said, "He seems like a good guy. Would you like to come get him so I don't have to haul him into detox?"

Alex got dressed and went on this sad, late-night errand. When Alex asked the officer how he had known to call us, he said that

Jeff had scrolled to "Timmy Home" on his cell phone and gave it to the officer to call. We all have times—lost, dark times—when we need to punch in "Home" and know we can get there. When we live in relationship, in networks of community, our homes provide safety nets for one another.

Community Strengthened through Crisis

Although none of us welcomes tragedy in our lives, there is a burnished beauty to a community that has suffered together. If you've been through such an experience—a natural disaster, perhaps—you know what I mean.

On April 20, 1999, the Colorado community where we live suffered the tragedy of the random killing of twelve students and a teacher in Columbine High School. It was an afternoon of horror and of the loss of innocence for two thousand students.

That evening, with our son Drew safely home from the ordeal, some good friends whose son had also been inside the school came over to our house. We ordered pizza, and we each called loved ones around the country on the landline and cell phones, and we kept close together. The TV traumatized us over and over until we realized there would be no new news and certainly no good news that night, and we turned it off, mostly because the kids didn't want to watch it.

A neighbor and his son came to the door and just stood in the front hall. I think they wanted us to interpret this for them and make sense of it. But we didn't have any words for that. It's not that we didn't have faith that somehow good would triumph. But words seemed small and trite.

The next morning a nesting instinct kicked in, and I knew the very first thing I needed to do was get more food into the house. No one would be going to work or school, and who knew what the day would bring? We needed to be prepared. *Get food,* I thought.

In the doorway of the supermarket, employees were giving away fresh doughnuts and coffee. Throughout the community, businesses expressed solidarity and sympathy in whatever simple ways they could.

The shootings were on a Tuesday, and it rained and snowed for the next several days. A newspaper headline read, "The Sky Wept." By Saturday our finished basement had flooded. Sometimes the proverbial straw breaks the camel's back, and we simply couldn't deal with the magnitude of the mess.

Alex was scoutmaster of a neighborhood Boy Scout troop. He made a phone call or two, and some of the older boys showed up at the door to help. They moved furniture and boxes and ripped up all the carpeting and pad and hauled it outside to the trash. (This wasn't the first time the basement had flooded, and this time the carpet wasn't worth saving.) They mopped the floor and set up fans in the basement. That night some friends who did not have students at Columbine took us out to dinner.

Sometimes your home systems get hit with a crisis that you just can't handle alone. And at such times it's a beautiful thing to accept help and have the network of a community that gladly provides it.

As the days, weeks, and months passed with a progression of new wounds and healings, this community bonded proudly and powerfully. The experience left us with a sense of being tattooed with the symbol of a columbine flower. We are marked forever, particularly our children. But there's tremendous strength in this community.

And those neighbor women whom I continue to walk with in the mornings, meeting on a corner at 6:00 a.m.? Kathy lost a nephew in the shootings. Terry lost the son of neighbors two doors over. The home of one of the killers is in our neighborhood too. Community is messy. But as we walk each morning and talk, we've grown to count on each other, knowing that ears are listening as our shoes hit the pavement. Each morning when we part for the day, we're a little richer because we've been together. We step a little lighter. For we are neighbors, in community.

Home Tour: Cathy's Heavenly Burritos

Cathy A. and Phil, who is a pastor, became increasingly alarmed as the local hangout house in the neighborhood became a drug house and their son and Phil's brother's son often hung out there. They gathered with Phil's brother's family. What could they do? Telling the boys they didn't want them at that house wasn't making any difference.

The adults decided it was time to intervene. But what could they do? Cathy had an idea. Her sister-in-law made the beans; Cathy made the chili. They shaped a big pile of burritos and prayed over them.

Then they took the burritos to the drug house door, offered them as a gift to the family who lived there, and said they would like to pray for them. The family was grieving the loss of a grandmother. The father put down his beer can and invited them in, and they all held hands and prayed.

The story of Cathy's Heavenly Burritos has a happy ending: The drug house isn't one anymore. The family there now attends Phil's church. Cathy and Phil's son is strong in faith, drug free, and an inspiration to other kids in the community.

Cathy says she believed she needed to start from square one and share the love of Jesus with them. She did it with what she knew how to share: burritos.

Working from Home

It's a Thursday morning, and today I have the luxury of reverting to my routine of many years: working from home. In contrast to my office at **MOPS** International (Mothers of Preschoolers), which is in the center of the building with no windows, from my home office I can glance out the window to my right and remember that it is late summer and the shrubbery is green. Traffic sounds and an occasional dog's bark travel to me on a breeze through the window. I have always been grateful that I can do work that I love (writing) from my grounded-in-life home while still connected to a larger world with all my long technological fingers.

When I worked daily from home, I faced the key challenge for anyone who works from a home office: How do you make your workplace in a place that is also where you play and rest? How do you make your play and rest place into the place where you also work? Working from home stretches that environment into multiple personalities. Do you want to make your home do that? Maybe you really do. But think through this carefully so these multiple personalities won't fight with each other.

Why Work from Home?

People have many different motives for working from home. If you are currently working from home, is it so that you can also stay at home with young children? Or to be independent, as your own boss, while expending little money on overhead? Is flexibility your prime motivation? Or perhaps you have a talent that thrives best in the environment of your home. Are you having difficulty finding employment "outside" and in the meantime are doing your best on work at home? Are you even escaping a more difficult world of work "out there"? If you are working from home or are thinking about working from home, you'll want to be clear in your own mind about why you are doing it.

Being clear in your own mind helps you be clear in explaining the "why" to the people you live with, all of whom need to flex around this "work personality" of home. You will need their respect, for one thing. Janie and her husband Bill operate a business from their home; Bill sets up appointments for Janie, who travels around the city performing on-site insurance medical exams. When they moved in with Janie's elderly father so that they could care for him, her father didn't believe that Bill "worked" because he wasn't out of the house from 9:00 to 5:00. Her father made digs at Bill, and Bill behaved in ways he knew would annoy Janie's father. Janie finally had to sit down with the two and say, "Dad, this is my husband. You're going to respect him. I'm not going to take sides. You two have to get along." And as time went by and her father had to depend upon Bill more each day to drive him to appointments and such—which Bill could do because he had a flexible schedule—the father softened and even said he was sorry.

By the same token, the one who works at home must be sensitive to family routines and dynamics. If you teach piano lessons at home, for example, this might not work well while your kids are doing their homework.

When the time was right in my life to transition from a home office to working outside the home, I joked to Alex that I could get a "real job." To his credit that wasn't his expression; it was mine. Family members need to feel like this *is* a "real job" in order for working at home, where family members rest and play, to be successful.

Another good question to ask yourself is whether you have a temperament that would thrive in a home environment. In general, a home work base will be easier for the introvert than for the extrovert, unless your business involves getting out of the home to visit with clients. Alex worked from home for a few years, but as an extrovert he required the balance of spending his hours outside of work being involved with lots of people, in his case a large Boy Scout troop. Gus the dog helped keep him company too. But as I looked at the row of dress shirts waiting dormant in his closet, I couldn't believe that working from home would last long for him, and it didn't.

Kathy C. learned that flexibility is crucial for the health of an at-home business, especially with one's spouse. "If you asked me fifteen years ago [what I thought about working from home], you would have gotten a different set of answers," said Kathy. "It was very stressful for me. I wanted more separation between business and home. I wanted to have a lot more things the way I wanted them to happen. I had to go through some major adjustments. I've come full circle to enjoy some of the things I didn't enjoy at all."

It's good to establish firmly in your mind why you're doing this and what adaptations are necessary to make it work.

What Kind of Work Are You Doing?

The variety of types of businesses that can be operated from home is about as wide as your imagination. Cynthia breeds Labrador puppies. Talk about a business that involves the whole fam-

WORK THAT CAN WORK FROM HOME

Here are a few of the many kinds of work that can happen from home:

bookkeeping

music lessons

photography

sewing and alteration

jewelry making

editing

data entry

counseling

dog grooming

interior design

catering

architecture

website design

ily and the home! The dining room is cordoned off and converted into the puppy nursery. The kids, who are fifteen, twelve, and five, can view puppies wriggling over each other, sleeping, playing, or nursing as they come and go through the house. The day the mother whelped her puppies, Cynthia let the kids stay home from school. They helped in many ways, like cutting umbilical cords and rubbing the puppies hard until they took their first breath. They tied a different color ribbon around each puppy's neck to identify him or her and kept careful records on each one.

Ginger, who has a new baby, chose architecture as a profession partly because she can work on designs and projects at home with her children. She's taken this plan into consideration in remodeling their old home so that she has an office with a play area, but it's removed enough from the baby's room that the baby can nap without hearing mom, and vice versa.

Steve P., who is a paraplegic, continually adapts his home. He says, "It's not just a place where I live; it's a place that really helps me function." His mom has given him a plaque that used to hang in her home that says "Home Sweet Home." It hangs prominently in Steve's family room. To help him function in the world of work, he has a long desk built in at the right height to accommodate his wheelchair, and from his home sweet home Steve does website design.

Meredith is a photographer specializing in photographing children and families. She has a studio in her basement. "It's nice to have something that's just mine," she says. "I can work when I want to or let it go for a while."

From a small studio converted from their first-floor den, Mary does manicures and facials. Anne keeps samples for her interior-design business in a converted upstairs bedroom and goes out of the home to see clients in theirs. Sharon gives violin lessons. So many types of work can be made to work at home.

Work Space at Home

One secret to success in working at home seems to be defining a space for work. This was important to Keri, who said, "When I first started writing, I had a laptop in my bedroom and didn't have an office. When we moved, my husband, who is a realtor, thought every wall should be beige. I claimed this space for my office. 'You get to go away to an office, but this is my space.' So I painted it green and texturized the walls, and got lamps that had colorful shades, and put pillows in one corner. I made it my space. I have bookshelves everywhere. It's my sanctuary. It's a place where I work, but it's also a place where I can shut the door and be myself. It gets a little messy in there because I'm not a neatnik. So there are papers piled sometimes and books piled, but it's space that's a blessing to me. A place where I do . . . what fuels me creatively."

Like when Keri first worked from a laptop in the bedroom, sometimes a makeshift arrangement has to suffice if you don't have the space or can't afford to decorate a room. For Brandy, who is a realtor, one special chair defines her work space. "When we moved the two girls to the basement bedroom," says Brandy, "we made the front bedroom an office. And I have a chair in there that's from the sixties or the seventies that was my husband's grandfather's. . . . It's just a very comfortable chair. It's kind of retro and fun because it still has the old green and gold fabric. That's where I like to sit when I read." If Brandy needs to share a home office with her husband, having at least this chair in the room just for her helps her have a sense of her own workplace.

Bruce transitioned from a job that involved nearly constant travel to working from a home office with no travel. The thing he loves most about their home, the thing that makes it possible for him to settle in and stay put, is a panoramic view of the front range of the Rocky Mountains. "Now I feel like we have this whole piece of nature that's part of our home," says his wife Shelly. "You can sit almost anywhere in my house and that's what you see. That's part of the landscape, part of the decorating; it's probably our favorite thing about the house."

Kathy D.'s family farms and ranches, so technically the entire family works from home. If you come in their back door, Kathy says, you can tell just how they make their living, because "uniforms" are collected there. Lining the floor and on pegs are their hats, coveralls, and boots used for working outside. "It's part of who we are," says Kathy. "I have a shovel by my back door so if there's a snake I can deal with it."

Working Smart from Home

Working smart at home is a logical part of maintaining a balance between work, play, rest, and home. It helps us preserve quality relational time. Paula has developed and built from her home a business designing miniature brass stencils and selling them all over the world. Her advice is to start small. "You can't do something like this overnight," says Paula. "You have to learn it a step at a time." She says to never take out a loan and to start in small increments. "Don't try to be a large corporation," she says. "Be what you are, a small home-based business, and grow gradually. Grow in the steps that you can. It becomes another child. You have to juggle another child. Let it grow naturally."

One of the significant challenges I noticed when I was working as a writer from my home is the need to develop an at-work mindset. When a friend calls, knowing full well that you're at home, and wants you to go out for coffee, you have to have a standard one-liner ready, like "I'm sorry, but I have an appointment then (with my computer)," or "I'm sorry, I'm booked that morning, how about (another time) instead." It helps to literally determine your working hours—and then you must stick with them. Sure, they need to be reevaluated over time as other responsibilities change, but having set hours helps.

The ability to multitask at home is a benefit of the home office, but it can also be an insidious way to rob you of being at your best on any side. One day I had the ultimate in multi-tasking breakdown: I was trying to write, the piano tuner was pounding notes in the living room a few feet away, men were trimming trees outside the open window, and another guy was cleaning the carpet in the family room. By the time the piano tuner complained, I was ready to run shrieking from the house. Just because you're working at home doesn't mean you should schedule to have too many things done at home at once. I think from the home's perspective, this would be like trying to have a massage and pedicure while you run on a treadmill!

Two important decisions for the at-home office are how to handle phone calls and whether to have clients visit you at home. Paula's experience is telling in both respects. Paula used to include her home address and phone number on stencil packaging. Now and then people showed up at the door to purchase stencils. But one day a scraggly, scary-looking man came to the door while Paula was working at home with her young children, and that was the end of the practice of publishing their home address and phone number.

Rebecca and Nathan both occasionally work from home in their small loft apartment. They've learned to be pretty direct with each other when they need some quiet time and space. If Nathan is on a freelance music project or Rebecca needs to sit on the sofa with her laptop and work for a few hours, they'll say, "You know, I need to focus for the next hour. Could you just leave me alone?" and that's okay. They also respect one another's space. Nathan's is a small music office; Rebecca's space is the kitchen.

Sara is a singer and songwriter who composes at home. "This piano that I got in college, an old upright Baldwin, inspires me. It has a warm, soft sound. I always write at home," says Sara. "I'm sterile on the road. There must be something about home. I always write at night. I love to come here after I clean the kitchen. The dishwasher is whirring away. You can look out the window at some trees."

Sara has learned from her mother, an elementary school principal, an important lesson about how she approaches her work. "My mom says that every student has a dance before they can do their work. They've got to sharpen their pencil or whatever they do. Some students' dance is long, some is short. Early on mine was identified as really, really long." Part of her dance is that she needs to clean up the kitchen in the evening; then she can write.

What about the Kids?

Juggling the care of young children is the most common challenge of the at-home entrepreneur. Keri used different strategies as her two children grew and their needs changed. When her daughter Melanie was a baby, Keri laid Melanie under her desk with interlocking links and hanging toys to occupy her. Keri moved the toys with her feet while she was typing. "When she was really little I was doing business writing," Keri said. She'd have the phone and a notebook and nurse the baby while she took a phone interview. "These businessmen . . . if they only knew," Keri said. "It's worth it to get a sitter at least for a few hours to work when they're small because you need to have some uninterrupted time or you get frustrated. . . . The quality of work suffers."

Keri also has used a babysitter in her home to play with her children and take them out in the backyard or to the park. "It's hard to set the boundaries between work time and what really should be family time," Keri said. "But it's important to decide the hours that you'll work and then stop when those hours are over."

Julie is a writer, and she gets as much written as she can while her daughter is in school and her son is in preschool for two and a half hours each morning. After that time she has to get creative. "They're very artistic, so in my office I have tons of art stuff, and they'll be perfectly content sitting there drawing or painting or doing puzzles or playing games with each other quietly at my feet while I am working. . . . I do as much as I can through email so I can interrupt an email real quick and help a puzzle piece fit. On the telephone it's harder because I never know when they're going to need me. Now that they're getting older, that's a lot easier too. A two-year-old, three-year-old doesn't understand *wait thirty minutes*, but now they do."

Brandy the realtor takes her daughters to a babysitter two days a week so she can have dedicated work time. "I do work at home, but just not having them around makes me able to get something done. When they're home, it's hard." Brandy schedules home showings on Tuesdays or Thursdays, when she has the girls with a sitter, or on Mondays or weekends because her husband can watch them then.

"I get up between 4:00 and 5:00 a.m. every day," says Paula, "and I work at night. I work like a fiend during school and play dates." Her husband does the laundry while she's at craft fairs and is willing to handle dinner. But as one of her kids said, "When Dad had to make dinner, that was bad. It was pizza out of the freezer."

Paula involved the kids from the beginning when she exhibited at packaging and craft shows. They demonstrated her stencil products, and Paula paid them by the hour, just as she would pay an adult. "Who better to draw people in than a four-, six-, eight-year-old demonstrating?" asked Paula. The kids played under the table with Barbies and came out enough to make it worthwhile. If you'd like to try this, remember that not all shows allow children. But some are family-friendly.

When Is It Time to Quit Working at Home?

Something about working from home, in the back and forth of family life, keeps us grounded and adds a unique awareness of what is important. But inherent in this lifestyle are difficult choices to be made continually between one priority and another. Work or rest? Work or play? Work only when the house is empty? Work when others are underfoot?

In the midst of this constant need to make choices, ruts can also deepen on the sly. Home is a spoiling environment: working in shorts and a T-shirt, lunches on the patio. Making up your mind to leave this environment can be like trying to get up from a too-deep, overstuffed sofa. It's good to evaluate periodically whether it is time to either come home for work or go out into the larger workplace again.

Evaluate realistically, from time to time, your goals for working at home, whether you are achieving them or will be able to, and how your work is impacting other family members and home life. Ask yourself whether your work enriches or significantly drains relationships and the home atmosphere. Working should be succeeding on multiple fronts if you're doing it at home.

Home Tour: Meredith's Photography Studio

When Meredith's first child Grace was an infant, Meredith worked three mornings a week for a wedding photographer to get out of the house a bit. Once she realized that she enjoyed photography and that she could be a photographer from her home, she started ordering backdrop sets for a basement studio.

Meredith specializes in photographing families and siblings, and the business has worked well both for her clients and for her own family—husband T. J. and young children Grace and Jackson.

She books sittings on evenings and Saturdays, with T. J. caring for the kids. Her mom takes the kids one day a week so that Meredith can run errands, clean the house, and generally catch up on work.

Her clients like the flexibility. "They can breast-feed over here for forty minutes and I don't care," says Meredith. "They can come get their orders at 9:00 p.m. after their kids are in bed." This is an important benefit over an outside studio. At the same time, Meredith works hard to keep the house clean and quiet so that the atmosphere is professional and comfortable.

"I like most getting to meet new families, new moms," says Meredith. "We share experiences; it makes you feel more normal." When Grace entered kindergarten, Meredith's business grew as other moms learned what she did. "When they find out they're like 'Ooooh. . . .' It's not like you're trying to get their business. They find out. It's cool that way," says Meredith.

Meredith's background in sales and merchandising is valuable. "It can be big if I put more time to it. I like it like it is now. When they're in school, I can put more work into it." Meanwhile, she's learning how to maximize her time, what facets of the work to send out, and how to cut corners. "It doesn't pay to put in too many hours and be grumpy the next day," she says.

The family has had evenings when a one-hour appointment becomes three and T. J. and the kids go out for fast food late or are waiting in the master bedroom. But T. J. enjoys the time with the kids. "We have a good time. We go swimming. There's a lot of stuff going on outside."

Home Tour: From Paula's Home to Europe and Beyond

Paula started as a quilter designing stencils for quilt patterns. She offered some of her designs to a company that called and wanted to buy them. Paula had the foresight to copyright them, so she received royalties on her designs.

Today Paula designs miniature brass stencils for quilts, stationery, and scrapbook pages and for use on paper, fabric, or wood. She has her own catalogs and manufacturer.

Along the way Paula has provided phenomenal experiences for her children and also for other moms she employs. As her children have grown, they have gone from helping her exhibit at craft shows to helping her on TV shows and creating advertising and their own designs. "Our kids have an incredible work ethic," Paula says. "They have been exposed to things most kids are never exposed to. We talk business at the dinner table, breakfast table, et cetera. They have been exposed to entrepreneurial business since they were tiny. I don't know that they'd ever want to step into the business, but they all could."

Once they were exhibiting at a large tradeshow in Chicago when two men walked up to the booth and talked with her daughter Jennifer, inviting them to come to England and do eight television shows. *Stencil Techniques with Paula*, which still airs, demonstrates seventeen different techniques. Paula likes to rotate her business trips so that she takes one of her three children with her each time. It's their time to hang out together.

At Home in the World

On Sunday evenings when I was growing up, my dad picked up my two grandmothers and brought them over for dinner. This was a special treat: my father picked up fat, juicy hamburgers at King's Food Host on his way home with "the G's." One of the grandmothers was chatty and participatory. The other one, whom I never felt like I really knew, sat in silence, taking everything in but not saying a word. I always wondered why Dad picked her up and brought her over. She didn't seem to be having a good time.

Now that I'm older, I think I understand. Grandma could sit alone and have hot chipped beef on toast (one of her favorites), or she could have a little heftier fare and take in our banter about school, work, and sports. Although she might not have shown it, we widened the small circle of her life, if just a little.

Living in a Wide Circle

We all know small-circle people and wide-circle people. Small-circle people have few and tightly focused interests and acquaintances. Wide-circle people have a wide-ranging curiosity and know people whose life experience is not closely related to their own. Small-circle people can have a satisfying home experience. And yet they also miss out on so much richness of life; they just usually don't know it.

At its healthiest, our home experience should fill us, settle us, and prepare us to launch out into wider circles that periodically bring us back home again for refueling and reconnecting.

The journey can start quite simply. Over many years our family has supported children around the world through Compassion International, an organization that meets basic needs for food and education for needy children in many countries. Although several of the children we've sponsored are young adults now and we have no contact with them, I like to look at their old photographs and pray for them: Ricardo in Ecuador, a handsome, responsible-looking young man; Bulalindo in Congo, whose eyes look like she has seen far too much for her age; Nathaniel in India, so very thin; Himanshu in India, at nine years old the youngest, standing tall and bright-eyed; Somjai in Thailand, who looks like a leader; Kyamazima from Rwanda, whose photo I lost—did she survive the genocide there?; and Edy from the Dominican Republic, who challenges me with his somber stare and makes me wonder what he would say to me. I wonder at their worlds and their everyday lives, and my own circle expands beyond the trips I made today to work and to the supermarket.

These are picture-children's worlds, but as parents our circles travel out with those of our children.

Our son Tim is an avid mountain biker, and one autumn Alex and I went to Moab, Utah, to cook meals for his mountain bike racing team, Team Ironclad. The race is ridiculous. It's called "24 Hours of Moab" and is a twenty-four-hour relay race. Each of four teammates rides his or her hour-and-a-half lap out in the mesa and canyons, then "passes the baton" to another teammate, and round and round it goes, including in the darkness

TOP 10 THINGS PEOPLE FROM OTHER COUNTRIES ENJOY IN AMERICA

the friendliness and openness of Americans

shopping at stores like Wal-Mart and Target

McDonald's

nobody's on the street (where is everybody?)

neighborhood cleanliness and quiet

the spaciousness of our homes

the wide variety of food

comfortable beds

separate bathrooms

Americans being kind to them if they can't speak English well

with miners' lights on their foreheads. It draws hundreds of crazy, avid bikers.

As a ministry, Team Ironclad offers warm soup to riders through the night. It was worth working the late night shift, preparing soup in huge pots on camp stoves in a large tent, and then sleeping in a small tent on an air mattress just to see the reaction to a warm bowl of soup offered without charge, in the middle of the night, in the midst of warm people. It was like "home" from a pot!

Another form of journeying wide took place in our own home with two college students, Michaela from Bari, Italy, and Anne from Finland. We signed up for a program through our church that matches families with international students at a local university to provide them with friendship and a touch of home.

The boys were in elementary school at the time. Throughout the meal, I guess we botched the pronunciation of Michaela's name pretty badly. He finally stopped us and said, "Look, other things don't matter, but my name is important to me. Could you please try to get it right?" We practiced with him, we practiced without him in the coming weeks, and I can guarantee you that we not only always thereafter got it right but also now all pay attention to how people from other places pronounce their names. It's a big little thing that matters.

Leona, who has been involved in local public office for many years, participates in a program hosting Russian leaders in her home for eight days to two months at a time. This is what she says about that experience: "When you think of the terrible fighting that goes on in the world, I think the only hope is getting to know people on a one-on-one basis. Once they stay in your guestroom and meet your family. . . . I remember a Russian who had only stayed in Washington, DC, and when he came here he said, 'I have found the real America.'" Leona continues, "The only way people really get to know each other is to come into our homes. Our homes are the most important. . . . It's where people should be the most open. Having guests can be the most natural thing, and it's the most humble thing in the world. You don't have to be concerned about getting out your best dishes or be concerned about the meal."

How does she handle serving meals to many people from a variety of cultures? "It seems like the older I get, the less stressed I am about it," she says. "In winter I make a big batch of soup and homemade bread. I can put on an elegant meal. I love it. I can spend a day setting the table. But my husband always says we have the most fun when I do it in a very simple way."

Keri, too, has learned that you don't have to wait until you live in an elegant home to have company from somewhere else. "We have a place in the basement where people can stay. It's ugly and has a half bath. You have to go two stories up to shower. There's a storage area in one end of the room. People from all over the world stay there [for pastors' conferences at her church]."

These experiences widen our circles, build understanding, and enrich our lives without a great deal of effort on our part other than being willing and eager to widen our circle.

Staying Connected to Home

Each year at Christmas we celebrate the Advent season, the coming of the Christ, on the four Sunday evenings before Christmas. We learned over the years to keep it very simple, so it consisted of lighting the candles in the Advent wreath, reading a portion of Scripture foretelling the birth of the Savior, singing a Christmas carol, and prayer. When Dan was away at college, we connected with him on a Sunday night during Advent via speaker phone. And it occurred to me as I listened to Dan's voice singing "O Little Town of Bethlehem" that his roommates and dorm neighbors must have gotten a chuckle. I was touched that he would do this out of a desire to stay connected with a Christmas tradition and with home.

When Drew went to college in Sterling, Kansas (population 2,000), care packages of favorite cookies and snacks from home were a premium. There was really no place for him to get treats other than the one supermarket or the Duckwall's Variety store downtown. He decorated his room with his assortment of hats and Broadway show posters, carrying forward into his new college life his "actor" identity that we knew well at home.

Alex and I had two choices for lodging when we went to visit Drew. One was the only motel in town, which sported signs for hunters: "Please don't wash your game in the sink." The other was Prairie Garden Bed-and-Breakfast, in a lovely restored Victorian home. We made reservations at the latter many months in advance. The charm of a bed-and-breakfast is in all the delightful touches of home: beds with quilts, a comfy place to read, a delicious breakfast with the host and hostess and other guests. People pay to stay at a B and B because it's like staying at home while they're away.

Whether we're staying at a B and B or a hotel, I have to unpack first thing—it's nesting, I guess—making this strange place home. When Mimi travels she packs a candle for hotel rooms and sometimes chocolate or a special treat. Allen kept in his pants pocket with his change four silver trinkets—Monopoly game piece size—to represent each of his four children. Whenever he put his hand into his pocket and felt one of the charms, he remembered and prayed for the child it represented. The preciousness of home is worth taking with us.

Launching Out into the World

When Dan was in high school, his soccer team traveled to Mexico City for a tournament and stayed in the homes of Mexican soccer players. Dan called one night, needing a connection back home. Dan spoke no Spanish, and his host family spoke no English. And that evening he had been served some sort of brains for dinner, which he ate. On the phone he recounted these facts. Then he paused. "Dan, you're all right, aren't you?" I asked. Another pause. "Yeah. I'm all right." Processing with us seemed to be enough; he would survive this adventure in a foreign place.

The biggest adventure of my life to date came in 1989, when I was invited to accompany Larry and Shirley Rascher on a nearly two-week trip to Irian Jaya on the island of New Guinea just north of Australia. The Raschers had been missionaries there for twenty years, part of the time living with primitive tribes in the swamps of the south coast, and I was writing their biography.

At the time I had three fairly young children, and I was afraid of flying (what would happen to the kids if I went down?), and I would be traveling separately from the Raschers. I cried all the way from Denver to Los Angeles, thinking I had surely lost my mind. Midway over the Pacific, I looked out into the darkness and saw the Big Dipper, perfectly framed by my square airplane window. I had the sense that God was saying to me, "I am pouring out my blessings on you," and I felt an overwhelming peace.

At the end of the fourteen-hour flight that had refueled in

Hawaii, it occurred to me that at the airport I was to meet their son, whom I had never met. If he wasn't there, I didn't speak any Indonesian and would have none of the right money for a phone call, if there were even telephones! But as the plane taxied up to the Quonset hut airport, standing out front I saw three slightly built Asian men and one tall blond. He was there.

This trip to Irian Jaya opened the world to me. I remained healthy throughout the trip, and I learned wonder after wonder as a completely different culture unfolded before me. If I could go to Irian Jaya, where couldn't I go? How about you? Where couldn't you go? Fewer places than you probably think!

Brittany spent a summer in Macedonia as a college student. She lived in a student dormitory in a town on the border between Albania and Macedonia as a member of a multicultural team. For Brittany this team became a close community and represented a sort of home. "It was a feeling of belonging," she said. "Like you knew these were people you could come back to. If you needed to talk, you could grab one of these people and say, 'I'm really struggling . . . do you want to get a coffee at the cafe?'

"We went around and shared our fears for the summer at the beginning," Brittany said. "So we were vulnerable, and it made us more approachable to each other, because we all knew we all have fears."

Coming Home Again

When we venture out and come back again, homecoming is sweet. Mimi was raised in the Congo in Africa, and when she returned after many years in the States, she told her mother, "That smell! I've missed that smell of home."

"Why, honey, that's mildew!" her mother said.

Whether it's mildew or lilac bushes, there's something about the smell and the sounds and the tastes of home. And we enrich the home brew as we bring back elements we've gathered from afar.

One of my favorite stories is *The Wind in the Willows*. In this story a mole leaves his home underground and becomes friends with a water rat he meets by the river, and they take off across the English countryside on the trail of the errant Toad. Many months later, in the nighttime, their journey takes them, unbeknownst to Mole, very close to his home:

> We others, who have long lost the more subtle of the physical senses, have not even proper terms to express an animal's intercommunications with his surroundings, living or otherwise, and have only the word "smell," for instance, to include the whole range of delicate thrills which murmur in the nose of the animal night and day, summoning, warning, inciting, repelling. It was one of these mysterious fairy calls from out the void that suddenly reached Mole in the darkness, making him tingle through and through with its very familiar appeal, even while yet he could not clearly remember what it was. He stopped dead in his tracks, his nose searching hither and thither in its efforts to recapture the fine filament, the telegraphic current, that had so strongly moved him. A moment, and he had caught it again, and with it this time came recollection in fullest flood.
>
> Home! That was what they meant, those caressing appeals, those soft touches wafted through the air, those invisible little hands pulling and tugging, all one way! Why, it must be quite close by him at that moment, his old home that he had hurriedly forsaken and never sought again, that day when he first found the river! And now it was sending out its scouts and its messengers to capture him and bring him in. Since his escape on that bright morning he had hardly given it a thought, so absorbed had he been in his new life, in all its pleasures, its surprises, its fresh and captivating experiences. How, with a rush of old memories, how clearly it stood up before him, in the darkness! Shabby indeed, and small and poorly furnished, and yet his, the home he had made for himself, the home he had been so happy to get back to after his day's work. And the home had been happy with him, too, evidently, and was missing him, and wanted him back, and was telling him so, through his nose, sorrowfully, reproachfully, but

with no bitterness or anger; only with plaintive reminder that it was there, and wanted him.[1]

No matter how far away we roam, a telegraphic current welcomes us home again. We can roam in ever-widening circles, knowing that when we circle back to home, we bring with us experiences to enrich our own appreciation of home, and sometimes guests to share it with us.

Home Tour: Home on a Tour Bus

When Sara is on a music tour with her husband and two young sons, they create in their bus that special place they need: a home.

First they get their rhythm going. Each day their schedule is the same: lunch at noon; sound check at 3:00 p.m.; dinner at 5:00 p.m.; concert at 7:00 p.m.; pull out at 11:00 or midnight. In between are spaces for them to explore the town or the area where they live that day.

Sara says they try to travel light, to not have much stuff with them on the road. But one thing that helps her older son feel settled is giving him a paper bag to fill however he wants. He carts it around with him and just feels better with his bag of stuff.

Each family member has their personal bunk that is like their own little cave at night. The boys have kid bunks with sports scenes and little lights. This reminds Sara of a favorite storybook from her childhood: *Sneakers, the Seaside Cat* by Margaret Wise Brown. Sneakers had a hook for his hat and a hook for his pants and a hook for his coat. Then he got into his little bunk and went to sleep. When she walked into her and Troy's room and saw three hooks across the top, she thought of Sneakers and his hooks.

"I love making big [spaces] out of little spaces," she says. Despite its size, the bus is comforting. It helps them pull away, keep priorities, and have a home.

Home Tour: At Home in Nature

Julie and Chuck and their two young children love to get out into nature to camp. A lot of the fun of it Julie describes as "just being." They can fill a day together skipping rocks in a lake, fishing, watching animals, or climbing rocks and exploring the forest on a hike.

They enjoy setting up camp in a remote place, or at least in a quiet corner of an established campground. It is the kids' mission to gather sticks and organize the campfire. "They will work for hours gathering the sticks and getting everything we need to build the fire, and they take so much pride in it," says Julie. When they finally light it up, they spend the evening sitting around the fire together, talking and roasting marshmallows.

There is a coziness to setting up a temporary home in the woods, away from distractions, and a sweet togetherness in sleeping in a tent, a camper, or even a rustic cabin.

The Best Home at Last

On a sultry July evening my extended family gathered at the home of my brother and sister-in-law in Topeka. We had come to town for my mother's funeral the next morning. The evening's buffet supper was like many over which my mother had reigned, impeccably dressed and with her crown of white hair, from her favorite chair in the living room. We missed her presence, while at the same time it permeated the room.

After dinner we spilled out onto the spacious lawn as darkness fell gently under huge oak trees. My brother's home had been the backdrop for so many of these family gatherings. It anchored us in place, in continuity of relationship, and in time. We walked and stood and talked in precious family tableaus. And I watched my grown children pursuing one of the joys of my childhood—chasing fireflies.

With my mother's passing, an era had ended. My brothers and I were now the oldest generation. It was our turn. Before us lay the task of learning to do life right and finish well for our families, in our homes. Fortunately, we had learned much from our mother's example.

And my mother . . . where was she now? Above the fireflies and the towering oaks, what was there? Is there a final home?

We don't think much about heaven until we need to be sure someone we love is safely there. Perhaps until the loss of a child or of a loved one tragically and unexpectedly throws us into a cave of grief, craving the assurance we will be with them again. Or until life becomes so burdensome here that we must shift focus and cling to, and hope for, a better beyond. We hope for our best home, together, in heaven, at the last.

What Is Heaven Like?

When Bonnie's daddy, whom she described as "an elegant Southern man with a beautiful *Gone with the Wind* accent," was dying of Alzheimer's, she had what she considers the privilege to "love him home." "I think it's been the most sacred thing I've ever been a part of other than childbirth," she said. "Because we're not home. We're not home here. I don't want to leave any time soon, but when it's time . . .

"I'm a big believer that heaven is going to be mind-blowing," says Bonnie. "I don't think we've really seen colors yet. I don't think we've really heard music yet. The new heaven and the new earth are just going to be staggering."

What can we know about heaven? So much about heaven is a mystery. But then, if the actual blueprints were given to us now, would we be too analytical and miss the sheer wonder of it? Or would we want to check in too quickly, before our rooms are ready?

The Scriptures give four images of heaven to tease our imaginations. One image embraces the word *paradise*, which means a garden, park, or forest. So in this sense heaven is a great, verdant park.

The second image is of a great city, the New Jerusalem. Its description in Revelation 21 is filled with symbolism—gates of gold, streets of pearl. Some kind of beautiful and glorious heavenly city awaits us.

The third image of heaven is cosmic. Scripture says God will create a new heaven and a new earth in which righteousness dwells, and we will rejoice and be glad. There will be a cosmos to explore. Jim, a pastor, says, "I love exploration. I think I'll have eternity to explore the variety of his created works. . . . I want to see all of it. I want to see all the new earth. But I also want to see all the new heavens. I want to see the galactic systems. To me that's incredibly exciting."

"What intrigues me," says Pastor Ken, "is that we will know one another. Our entities will survive. But we'll have glorified bodies, similar to that of Christ."

Moving Up to the Big House

A fourth image of heaven comes from a description that Jesus shared with his closest disciples during the final week of his life on earth. He comforted them with this picture of a re-gathering with him in heaven:

> In my Father's house are many rooms; if it were not so, I would have told you. I am going there to prepare a place for you. And if I go and prepare a place for you, I will come back and take you to be with me that you also may be where I am.
>
> John 14:2–3

My friend Mimi, who has lived in the Middle East, says that in Middle Eastern cultures, the father owns the big house, and the sons add on rooms to his house. What a beautiful picture! God, whom the psalmist calls our dwelling place, will provide me some special "lodging" with him, with lots of terrific company. I've already been invited to move in. Jesus extended the invitation to me and will have the room ready and the night-light on when the time is right. I've sent my RSVP.

I will be at home forever and ever in a room in God's house that's complete and perfect and no doubt decorated tastefully and whimsically, as home was meant to be. The longing for home in my heart is satisfied a little bit when driving through Kansas prairies, a little bit at the old cabin in the mountains, and a little bit in the dwelling I live in now—but then it will be completely healed and filled. All pangs of homesickness will vanish when the home we've always longed for is ours forever.

But until that day, home here is a picture of what is possible. It is the key site of all the best loving and launching that happens in life. We continue constructing our homes here with a blueprint vaguely in view. It's not in focus clearly enough to be complete, but it's enough to give us the pattern, enough to encourage us to keep building.

The home our souls long for here provides a place where we're accepted as we are. It contains beauty and the comfort of favorite things, and it is a safe and stimulating place to work and to express creativity. We are nourished at the table with food and conversation, and we enjoy healthy life rhythms of play and rest. At home we have the opportunity to take care of things entrusted to us and to grow in spiritual understanding. We enjoy the legacy of generations and family celebrations. We treasure a place to build friendships and a base from which we can venture into the larger world and return. We will never have home just right this side of heaven, but we can keep changing and remodeling it through life seasons and circumstances. There's no work more rewarding.

Shari's heart longing is that her home reflects the best home to come. "A home that is warm and inviting and has a sense of humor shows a God that is the same," she says. "I want people to walk in this house and say, 'There is something I want to know about this family and ultimately about their God.'"

On the morning of my mother's funeral, family members were escorted from a limousine through the side door of the cathedral into a chapel. We waited there for others attending the funeral to be seated in the adjacent sanctuary. My mother had been the first infant baptized in this Episcopal cathedral, and she attended this one church her entire eighty-six years.

As we sat quietly in the chapel waiting, the organist in the sanctuary began playing the glorious pipe organ. And he played, of all things, *Claire de Lune* by Debussey, my mother's favorite piece. She had often told me that she had loved to play it on the piano when she was young.

Sun streamed through the stained glass windows, yet the high-ceilinged stone room was cool. I felt completely private in my thoughts of my mother, appreciating special memories of her life and of who she was to me. Listening to this organ piece was more her memorial for me than was the ensuing service.

At the conclusion of the day, back at my brother's home, I thanked him sincerely for asking the organist to play *Claire de Lune*. "To play *what*?" he asked.

So I went to my sister-in-law. She knew the organist, and surely, then, she had asked. "No, I didn't ask the organist to play anything," she replied.

Mystery. We have a mysterious God who loves us uniquely and individually. He wants to bless us at home here and here-after—and give us glimpses that connect the two.

Long ago, the apostle Paul wrote in a letter to one of the first groups of believers that they would be utterly amazed at what God is preparing for people who love him. He said they'd never seen nor heard nor even imagined anything like it (see 1 Cor. 2:9).

We have a home ahead that is wonderful beyond our paltry imaginings. Until we reach the Father's big house, we have the rewarding and ever-changing adventure of creating a place here for our souls to call home.

Home Tour: The House of the Lord

The LORD is my shepherd, I shall not be in want.
He makes me lie down in green pastures,
he leads me beside quiet waters,
he restores my soul.
He guides me in paths of righteousness
for his name's sake.
Even though I walk
through the valley of the shadow of death,
I will fear no evil,
for you are with me;
your rod and your staff,
they comfort me.
You prepare a table before me
in the presence of my enemies.
You anoint my head with oil;
my cup overflows.
Surely goodness and love will follow me
all the days of my life,
and I will dwell in the house of the LORD
forever.

Psalm 23

Home Tour: Our Dwelling Place

Lord, you have been our dwelling place
throughout all generations.
Before the mountains were born
or you brought forth the earth and the world,
from everlasting to everlasting you are God.

Psalm 90:1–2

Acknowledgments

The process from a dream to a book requires much from the people close to the author. A person with a dream can be obnoxious—have you noticed? They are driven and self-focused (or at least dream-focused). Rather than being available to family, friends, and colleagues as they once were, they are draining and driveling, talking incessantly about their topic.

So acknowledgments are important. They truly are.

For a book such as *Dwelling*, I guess I should start at the beginning, thanking grandparents and parents who provided for me a comfortable and enriching home. I admit it, I am blessed—spoiled even—but also grateful. All of these people have died. This makes me the more thankful for my brothers, Don and David Chubb, with whom I can reminisce about our parents, our grandparents, and our growing-up home.

The support of my colleagues at MOPS International (Mothers of Preschoolers) was crucial in nurturing my dream and propelled me forward, in particular Elisa Morgan, Craig Ellsworth, Carla Foote, Rachel Ryan, Jackie Alvarez, and Stephanie Rich.

My writer's critique group buddies cared enough to tell me when my writing was bad and to help me make it better: Jeanne

Dennis, Shelly Stieg, Lindsey O'Connor, and especially Kathy Groom, who relentlessly kept me to my best.

The seventy-five interviewees whom you met in the book lent invaluable insight. I've promised to quote them only by their first names, so I will not list them. But picture a room filled with seventy-five unique and special men and women, each adept at *dwelling*. Perhaps this will give you a sense of my gratitude and the magnitude of their contribution.

Here are other people who played particular, important parts: Gary Sokol, Katherine Williams, Cori Peth, Tracie Morton, Meredith Rikli, Jess Stainbrook, Kendall Parkhurst, and Susan Wallace.

It takes a creative, invested team to launch a book, and I couldn't ask for a better one: literary agent Lee Hough, and the team at Revell, especially Jennifer Leep, Twila Bennett, Suzie Cross, and Dave Lewis.

My family has contributed the most in this venture. Not just supporting me in the out-of-balance season of writing but in the *living* of the material. I am eternally blessed that we have dwelt together, in good times and hard ones: my husband Alex, Tim, Dan and his wife Stephanie, and Drew. Alex and I get to visit the guys in their own homes now. How fun is that!

If you have met Dr. Cal and Mimi Wilson, you will understand how indebted I am to them, especially my friend and business partner, Mimi. The Wilsons have made their home on a Native American reservation and in Congo, Jordan, Peru, Ecuador, and, fortunately for me, Denver. I know no better example of a "full circle home" than theirs. I've been privileged to visit their home, to watch, to learn.

Each of these has contributed their unique talents and personalities to what has become *Dwelling*. And I am very grateful.

Discussion Questions

Chapter 1 A Place to Be Me

1. What are the first things you do to "settle in" when you come home?
2. Summarize the personalities of those who live in your home. Where do you see thumbprints of each of these personalities in your home?
3. What potential challenges are posed by personality differences in your home? In what ways do the personalities in your home potentially balance one another?
4. If you have a father, a mother, and at least one child living in your home, summarize any differences between "Daddy style" and "Mommy style" of parenting. Are these right or wrong or just different? How does your child benefit from both?
5. Play back in your head a tape of the tone of voice that you've used in your home in the last twenty-four hours. Does it sound like the tone you would want others to use with you? If not, how can you be more aware of your tone and make it more positive?

Chapter 2 Beauty, Comfort, and Favorite Things

1. Describe homes you've been in that you think are beautiful.
2. What are some elements common to those homes?
3. What are some of your favorite things? Share the story behind one of them.
4. What senses are involved in your favorite memories of your home?
5. Describe something in your home that is beautiful to you.
6. At dinner tonight, ask your family members about their favorite things in your home. Consider whether you are giving respectful treatment to others' favorite things.
7. In what ways do you find yourself comparing your home with friends' homes and coming up short?
8. What are some of the positives, the blessings, of your home?
9. What are your observations about contentment?

Chapter 3 My Space, Our Space, and Creativity

1. What is the coziest space in your home?
2. What is the space in your home where your family most enjoys being together?
3. Describe any space in your home that you would like to arrange or use differently.
4. Tell about the part of your home that your husband would consider "his space," if he has such a space. What would you consider "your space"?
5. Do you have challenges in getting all family members to participate positively together? Have you found solutions that have worked for you?

6. Tell about a way in which you are creative. Perhaps it's not a "typical" expression of creativity.

7. Share your own feelings, positive or negative, about your sense of your mother's presence in your home during your childhood.

Chapter 4 Dining In

1. What are some of your favorite foods, and what are some good associations you have with them?

2. What do you think makes regular family mealtimes so powerfully positive for family members?

3. What does dinnertime typically look like at your house? Who cooks? What do you typically eat? What are the biggest challenges to preparing family meals? How have you tackled these challenges?

4. Would you say you employ any form of meal planning? If so, what do you do and how helpful is this system?

5. Imagine your family sitting around a table eating dinner. What typically makes this time fun? What makes it not fun?

6. What are some fun questions that you could "put on the table"?

7. Share a time when you were embarrassed because you didn't know the correct manners. Or share a time when you were relieved because you did.

8. What strength can you identify that eating together has given your family?

Chapter 5 Play and Rest

1. What room of your home is the place where people in your family play most? What makes that room conducive to play?
2. What is one way that you personally play at home?
3. What is one way that your family plays together at home?
4. What is one way that you rest at home?
5. What is one way that you rest at home as a family?
6. Which is harder for you, to play or to rest? Why?
7. Which do you think you need more of in your life, play or rest? Why?
8. Do you have a family pet? Does this pet help family members play or rest? If so, how?
9. Does your family have any regular set-aside times of rest at home? If so, what do they typically look like?

Chapter 6 Home Keeping

1. On a scale of one to five, with one being extremely messy and five being a perfectionist, where would you rate yourself on messy-to-perfectionist house cleaning style?
2. Are you more or less messy than most of your friends? Does this bother you? Should it?
3. If you are married, in what ways do you and your spouse approach cleaning and home chores similarly? Differently? How do you determine who will tackle which tasks?
4. Do you have particular cleaning routines or strategies that work for you that you could share?
5. If your children are old enough to have some home

chores, do they? How do you approach this, and how is it working?

6. What are some ways in which help is available to you? How readily do you ask for help?

7. What home maintenance project or household repair have you been involved in recently? What did you learn from this experience?

8. Have you experienced a happy side of housework? Explain.

Chapter 7 Geography of Home

1. Other than where you currently live with your family, where would you call home?

2. Tell about any "map" you have in your heart of a particular state, region, or country.

3. Describe the natural environment of your home. What is best about it? What would you like to improve?

4. What are some of your favorite sights, smells, sounds, and touches in nature? Do you associate any of these with home?

5. Tell about a time you've experienced a disaster. Did it affect your home? How?

6. Share a time that your home provided welcome shelter from extremes or storms.

7. Share a seasonal family tradition or one way you decorate your home for a particular season.

Chapter 8 Generations, Celebrations, and the Changing Nest

1. Talk about a celebration that has taken place in your home with extended family members. What was best and what was most difficult about this event?

2. How does your relationship with your mother differ when you are together in your home versus in her home versus in a neutral location?

3. Share some sensory memories (smell, taste, touch, sight, sound) about an older relative's home. What sort of emotions and memories do these evoke?

4. What are some of your home's best resources that you can use for a family celebration?

5. Share a favorite family tableau, a time when two or three family members were particularly enjoying each other.

6. Do you have friends in your life whom you have adopted, or could adopt, as "family"? If so, tell us a little about them.

7. What are some values that your family has established regarding the celebration of a major family holiday? Were these values challenged by other family members? If so, what happened?

8. Share any family tradition that is in danger of being given up. Do you have other traditions to take its place?

9. What has been your experience with moving? What has helped you feel at home in a new place?

10. What have you observed about transitions when your family or your family of origin has added or lost family members living at home?

Chapter 9 Having Company

1. What are some of your strong suits as a hostess—for example, foods you enjoy preparing?

2. What are some strong suits of your home that you can capitalize upon when you have company?

3. Tell about a time when you were a guest in a home and

felt particularly comfortable. Why do you think you felt so at home?

4. What questions can you think of that would make good table talk discussion questions? Remember, they must have no right or wrong answer, and it should be a question to which anyone will have an answer.

5. Have you ever had houseguests stay for a week or more? What was challenging about this, and what did you find helpful?

Chapter 10 At Home in Community

1. Do you have any friends in your neighborhood? If so, how did you get to know them?

2. What are your observations about how and where people get to know each other in the neighborhood in which you live?

3. Compare and contrast your current neighborhood with the one where you grew up.

4. If someone was a good neighbor to you, what would that look like? What sort of things would they do or not do?

5. Share any challenges you have with neighborhood children and any solutions.

6. Discuss Kim's comment that "community is messy and it's slow." Has this been your experience with any type of community? Explain.

7. Share a little about a community in which you are involved. What led you to this involvement? What is most satisfying about it? What is most difficult about it?

8. Tell about a time when you needed the "safety net" of another home or when you were able to provide one for others in your home.

Chapter 11 Working from Home

1. Are you currently working from home, have you worked from home in the past, or do you have a spouse who is working from home? If so, what sort of work is it and why from home?
2. Do you have a temperament that would thrive or is thriving in a working-from-home scenario? Explain.
3. Share a work-from-home situation that you've observed that seems to be working out well.
4. If you are working from home or doing projects from your home, describe the space you're using for this. What are the positive and negative aspects of this space?
5. Have you developed some strategies that help you work smart from home?
6. What child care strategies enable you to work from home or have you seen work for a friend who is working from her home?
7. As you look forward, do you see yourself joining the workforce or changing your work situation? What work situation looks appealing to you?

Chapter 12 At Home in the World

1. Share an experience in your life that stretched you to a "wider circle" experience with people or in places foreign to you.
2. How were you enriched by that experience?
3. Have you ever had a guest in your home from another country? Tell about that experience.
4. Have you ever been a guest in the home of someone of a different ethnicity or from another country? If so, what were some highlights of that experience?

5. Have you ever been outside the United States? Tell about the farthest place you've been.

6. Where is one place in the world that you would find interesting to visit? Why? What would you like to do there?

7. When you travel, do you find yourself "nesting" to create a sense of home? If so, in what ways do you do this?

8. Tell about a time that you were homesick. Where were you? What was it you missed?

Chapter 13 The Best Home at Last

1. What would your dream home look like—the place and the relationships?

2. Are elements of your dream home attainable here, someday? Are some elements not attainable in this life but a picture of what heaven might be? Explain.

3. What circumstance in your life has made you most wonder about and hope for heaven?

4. Talk about mystery. What are some things that are a mystery to you? Are you comfortable with mystery or not? Discuss.

5. If you care to do so, share your own imaginings of what heaven is like.

6. Examine Jesus's description of heaven in John 14:2–3. What do we learn about heaven from him here?

Notes

Introduction: The Home Tours Begin

1. Sarah Messer, *Red House: Being a Mostly Accurate Account of New England's Oldest Continuously Lived-in House* (New York: Penguin, 2005), 103.

Chapter 2: Beauty, Comfort, and Favorite Things

1. Donald Miller, *Blue Like Jazz: Nonreligious Thoughts on Christian Spirituality* (Nashville: Thomas Nelson, 2003), 190.

Chapter 3: My Space, Our Space, and Creativity

1. Kent Haruf, *Plainsong* (New York: Vintage Books, 1999), 132–33.
2. George Howe Colt, "The Awakening," *Real Simple*, September 2005, 83.
3. Margaret Wise Brown, *Good Night Moon* (New York: HarperCollins, 1947).
4. Rick McKinley, *Jesus in the Margins: Finding God in the Places We Ignore* (Sisters, OR: Multnomah Publishers, 2005), 135.

Chapter 4: Dining In

1. Miriam Weinstein, *The Surprising Power of Family Meals* (Hanover, NH: Steerforth Press, 2005), 1–2.
2. Mimi Wilson and Mary Beth Lagerborg, *Once-a-Month Cooking* (New York: St. Martin's Press, 2007).
3. Edith Schaeffer, *Hidden Art* (Wheaton, IL: Tyndale House Publishers, 1971), 126.

Chapter 6: Home Keeping

1. Jeff Campbell and The Clean Team, *Speed Cleaning* (New York: Dell Publishing, 1991).

Chapter 7: Geography of Home

1. Elizabeth Weil, "Paradises Found," *Real Simple*, August 2005, 64.

2. Nessa Rapoport, *House on the River: A Summer Journey* (New York: Harmony Books, 2004), 113.

3. See for example Kathleen Norris, *Dakota: A Spiritual Geography* (Boston: Houghton Mifflin, 1993); Eudora Welty and William Maxwell, *One Time, One Place: Mississippi in the Depression: A Snapshot Album* (1971; repr., Oxford, MS: University Press of Mississippi, 1996); and Wallace Stegner, *Beyond the Hundredth Meridian: John Wesley Powell and the Second Opening of the West* (1954; repr., New York: Penguin Books, 1992).

4. Alexander McCall Smith, *The No. 1 Ladies' Detective Agency* (New York: Anchor Books, 1998), 18.

Chapter 10: At Home in Community

1. Michele Norris, "Porches Knit Together New Urbanist Communities," National Public Radio, *People and Places*, August 2, 2006.

2. McKinley, *Jesus in the Margins*, 158.

3. Jacquelyn L. Tobin and Raymond G. Dobard, Ph.D., *Hidden in Plain View: A Secret Story of Quilts and the Underground Railroad* (New York: Doubleday, 1991), 70.

Chapter 12: At Home in the World

1. Kenneth Grahame, *The Wind in the Willows* (New York: Galahad Books, 1982), 57–58.

You take care of your children, mom. Who takes care of you? MOPS International (Mothers of Preschoolers) encourages, equips, and develops mothers of preschoolers to be the best moms they can be.

MOPS is dedicated to the message that "mothering matters," and understands that moms of young children need encouragement during these critical and formative years. Chartered MOPS groups meet in approximately 4,000 churches and Christian ministries throughout the United States and 24 other countries. Each MOPS group helps mothers find friendship and acceptance, provides opportunities for women to develop and practice leadership skills in a group, and promotes spiritual growth. MOPS groups are chartered ministries of local churches and meet at a variety of times and locations: daytime, evenings, and on weekends; in churches, homes, and workplaces.

The **MOPPETS** program offers a loving, learning experience for children while their moms attend MOPS. Other quality MOPS resources include *MOMSense* magazine, MOPS books available at www.MOPShop.org, web site forums, and events.

With 14.3 million mothers of preschoolers in the United States alone, many moms can't attend a MOPS group. However, these moms still need the mothering support that MOPS International can offer. For a small registration fee, any mother of a preschooler can join the MOPS International Membership and receive *MOMSense* magazine (6 times a year), a weekly MOM-E-Mail of encouragement, and other valuable benefits.

Get Connected!
www.MOPS.org

Mary Beth Lagerborg is director of media for MOPS International (Mothers of Preschoolers), where for several years she has helped shape books, a magazine, and electronic media to meet the needs of moms and their families. She has written several books, including co-authoring the bestselling *Once-a-Month Cooking*, and speaks on topics related to creating a home. She and her husband Alex have three grown sons and make their home in Littleton, Colorado.

Inspiration for women

Gentle, practical advice on how to make time for what matters most. Includes "breathing" exercises.

A devotional that helps you take a deep breath for your soul, incorporating spiritual disciplines into your everyday life.

Just for moms

With warmth and vulnerability, Elsa Kok Colopy comes alongside readers as a trusted friend to help them handle twenty crucial single parenting issues.

Beth Vogt offers encouragement and wisdom to the growing demographic of later-in-life moms—whether through birth or adoption—from a mom who's been there.